one-pot
recipe collection

by **Sainsbury's**

100 delicious no-fuss family recipes

Welcome...

...to the one-pot recipe collection by Sainsbury's. We've put together a fantastic selection of brilliant dishes to give you everyday inspiration for easy one-pot meals. Each delicious recipe takes just 15 minutes or less in prep time, and has been tried, tested and tasted by Sainsbury's, so you can be sure of great results, whatever your level of cooking expertise. All the dishes are made from readily available ingredients with simple-to-follow, step-by-step instructions.

Most of the recipes in this book are all-in-one meal solutions; others are served with simple sides, such as ready-prepared salads, vegetables or rice that you can pick up in Sainsbury's and pop into the microwave to help make your life that much easier.

The recipes are divided into clear sections from soups to puddings, so it's easy to find just what you need to feed your family. They're arranged in each chapter from the speediest to the slowest, so you can choose just how much time you want to spend in the kitchen.

We hope you find plenty of inspiration to recreate and enjoy some of your all-time favourite dishes and this book becomes an indispensable addition to your kitchen. Happy cooking!

We've added icons to make everything as clear as possible:

 Suitable for vegetarians

 Recipes containing 1 or more of your 5-a-day, to help you plan for healthier eating. Aim to eat at least 5 different portions of fruit and veg a day. Fresh, frozen, dried, canned and juice all count.

contents

One-pot essentials...

Creating meals in one-pot makes cooking simpler, but you still need the right pots and pans for the job. You'll find an array of cookware instore or online at **sainsburys.co.uk** to help you make these recipes. Here's your go-to kit list:

Wok

With its smaller surface-to-hob area, this pan transfers heat quickly making it ideal for cooking fast and easy stir fries.

Frying pan

A shallow flat-bottomed pan for frying. For maximum versatility, buy one that's non-stick and ovenproof for total hob to oven capability.

Heavy-bottomed pans

A good set of solid pans is a kitchen must. A heavy base will conduct heat evenly so there's less risk of burning during cooking.

Steamer

Cooks veg and fish quickly while retaining moisture and essential nutrients. Comes separately or as part of your pan set to fit over the pots.

Roasting tin

Ideal for roasting meat and all the trimmings as well as whole fish. Look out for non-stick versions and tins with racks.

Baking dish

These are generally ceramic or made from heatproof glass and are ideal for baking savoury dishes and desserts.

Stockpot

A high sided pan with a lid used for making stock from scratch.

Casserole

A casserole is ideal for slow cooking. Get one that's flame- and ovenproof so it can be used on the hob and in the oven.

Griddle pan

A shallow ridged pan for frying or searing that gives food a lovely chargrilled effect and extra flavour.

Baking tray

A rectangular non-stick tray with shallow sides that's ideal for baking bread or cakes as well as baking fish.

Little pots

Ovenproof ceramic or glass pots are great for sweet or savoury individual portions and look pretty for presentation.

Tagine

A traditional Moroccan pot with a tapered lid to allow moisture to condense back into the dish during cooking.

soups

Serves 4
Prep time: 5 mins
Cook time: 10 mins

Ready in 15 mins

Quick spring minestrone

Tiny pasta and ready-chopped veg make this really quick to cook.
Serve with some crusty bread on the side for a simple but tasty meal

---

105g pack smoked pancetta for cooking by Sainsbury's
1 tbsp olive oil
1.2 litres chicken stock, hot
150g tub Sainsbury's Italian green pesto

125g conchigliette pasta, or any very small pasta shapes
600g frozen mixed special vegetables by Sainsbury's
Basil leaves, to garnish (optional)

---

1 Roughly chop all but 4 of the pancetta strips. Heat the oil in a large saucepan and fry both the chopped pancetta and whole pancetta strips for 3-4 mins until crisp. Remove from the pan and drain on kitchen paper. Set aside.

2 Add the stock to the pan with half of the pesto. Bring to the boil, then add the pasta, frozen vegetables and the fried chopped pancetta. Simmer, with the lid on, for 5 mins until the veg and pasta are tender. Season with salt and freshly ground black pepper to serve.

3 Divide between 4 bowls. Swirl a spoonful of the remaining pesto into each bowl, then top with a strip of crisp pancetta and a few basil leaves (if using).

Per serving: 472 cals, 27.8g fat, 7.3g sat fat, 3.5g total sugars, 2.1g salt

Cook's tip
Make this vegetarian – and even speedier – by leaving out the pancetta and using vegetable stock in place of the chicken stock.

Ready in 15 mins

Spicy Thai soup

This hot and fragrant noodle soup packs in a lot of delicious flavours – and plenty of prawns – in very little time!

Serves 4
Prep time: 5 mins
Cook time: 10 mins

2 tbsp Thai red curry paste
200ml reduced-fat coconut milk
750ml vegetable stock, hot
1 tbsp fish sauce
1 tsp light brown soft sugar
180g pack raw peeled
king prawns by Sainsbury's
300g pack mixed pepper
stir fry by Sainsbury's

5 spring onions, trimmed and finely sliced
300g pack rice noodles by Sainsbury's
Zest and juice of 1 lime
½ x 31g pack fresh coriander
by Sainsbury's, chopped,
plus extra leaves to garnish
50g young spinach

1 Heat a deep frying pan over a medium heat. Add the curry paste and cook for 1 min. Add the coconut milk, stock, fish sauce and sugar. Bring to the boil, then reduce the heat and simmer for 2 mins.

2 Add the prawns and cook for a further 2 mins. Add the stir fry vegetables, spring onions, rice noodles and the lime zest. Simmer for 2-3 mins, until the prawns are cooked through and piping hot. Stir in the lime juice and chopped coriander.

3 To serve, divide the soup between bowls, then add the spinach and garnish with the extra coriander leaves.

Per serving: 269 cals, 13g fat, 5.5g sat fat, 7.1g total sugars, 2.8g salt

Cook's tip
You can make this dish heartier by adding pieces of salmon or haddock at the same time as the prawns. The fish will take on all the delicious Thai flavours, and cook in minutes.

*Fast and filling
with a satisfying
dash of heat*

Serves 4
Prep time: 10 mins
Cook time: 20 mins

Ready in 30 mins

Salmon pho

Pho is a fragrant, flavoursome noodle soup from Vietnam that makes a great lunch or light supper. This speedy version is ready in just 30 mins

2 litres vegetable stock, hot
Knob of peeled fresh ginger (about 30g), sliced thinly
2 red chillies
10 spring onions, finely chopped
2 tbsp light soy sauce
2 x 200g packs Sainsbury's pak choi, quartered

2 x 240g packs boneless salmon fillets by Sainsbury's, skin removed and cut into chunks
2 x 300g packs rice noodles by Sainsbury's
Fresh mint and basil leaves, to serve

1 Put the vegetable stock in a large saucepan with the sliced ginger, 1 halved red chilli, the spring onions (reserving a tablespoonful for garnish) and soy sauce. Bring to the boil, then turn down the heat and simmer for 15 mins.

2 Remove the ginger and chilli from the broth and discard, then add the pak choi and salmon to the pan and cook for 3 mins.

3 To serve, divide the rice noodles between 2 serving bowls, then ladle over the pho. Garnish with the fresh mint and basil leaves, the remaining red chilli, deseeded and finely sliced, and the reserved spring onions.

Per serving: 438 cals, 16g fat, 4g sat fat, 4.6g total sugars, 2.4g salt

Cook's tip
If you like, you could add more veg to this dish – just add them in with the pak choi and salmon.

Ready in 40 mins

Mexican chilli bean soup

Serves 4
Prep time: 15 mins
Cook time: 25 mins

A smattering of dark chocolate gives this beany soup a lovely hint of sweetness. Serve with tortilla chips for the full Mexican experience!

1 tbsp olive oil
1 onion, roughly chopped
2 celery sticks, trimmed and sliced
2 carrots, peeled and diced
1 red pepper, deseeded and diced
2 cloves garlic, crushed
½ tsp paprika
1 red chilli, finely sliced
390g carton Italian chopped tomatoes in tomato juice by Sainsbury's

410g tin black-eyed beans by Sainsbury's, drained and rinsed
420g tin red kidney beans in chilli sauce by Sainsbury's
600ml vegetable stock, hot
50g dark chocolate, grated
5 spring onions, trimmed and finely sliced
1 lime, cut into wedges, to serve
4 tbsp soured cream, to serve

1 Heat the oil in a large saucepan and add the onion, celery, carrots and pepper. Cook over a medium heat for 10 mins, until the veg is soft. Add the garlic, the paprika and half of the chilli for the last 2 mins.

2 Stir in the tomatoes, the black-eyed beans and the kidney beans in chilli sauce. Pour in the stock, then simmer for 10 mins.

3 Sprinkle over the grated chocolate and stir though the spring onions. Divide between 4 bowls or mugs, and scatter over the remaining chilli. Season with salt and freshly ground black pepper and serve with the lime wedges and the soured cream on the side.

Per serving: 381 cals, 12g fat, 6g sat fat, 24g total sugars, 1.8g salt

Cook's tip
This is a great vegetarian recipe, but you could also try adding pieces of leftover roast chicken or beef.

Serves 4
Prep time: 5-10 mins
Cook time: 35 mins

Ready in 45 mins

Sweetcorn chowder with prawns

Chowder is a great comfort food dish that's really simple to make. Like most soups, you can vary the ingredients, depending on what you have to hand

2 tsp olive oil
1 tsp unsalted butter
1 onion, finely chopped
1 clove garlic, sliced
1 tsp Dijon mustard
½ tsp paprika
2 tbsp plain flour
500ml vegetable stock, hot
2 potatoes, peeled and cut into small cubes

2 x 325g tins naturally sweet sweetcorn by Sainsbury's, drained and rinsed
300ml semi-skimmed milk
100ml single cream
180g pack peeled raw king prawns by Sainsbury's
½ x 28g pack fresh flat-leaf parsley by Sainsbury's, chopped

1 Heat the oil and butter in a large pan. Add the onion, garlic, mustard and paprika and fry for about 5 mins, until softened.

2 Sprinkle in the flour and stir until absorbed. Remove from the heat and add the stock in batches, stirring until smooth each time. Return to the heat and add the potatoes.

3 Bring to the boil, then reduce the heat and simmer, stirring occasionally, for 10-15 mins until the potatoes are cooked. Add the sweetcorn and simmer for a further 5 mins.

4 Pour in the milk and cream, then add the prawns. Heat for about 5 mins, until the prawns are pink and cooked through.

5 Stir through the chopped parsley. Season with salt and freshly ground black pepper and serve.

Per serving: 353 cals, 11g fat, 5.1g sat fat, 18g total sugars, 2g salt

Ready in 45 mins

Malaysian chicken soup

Serves 4
Prep time: 15 mins
Cook time: 30 mins

Fresh lime, coriander and mint give this soup its zingy flavour. Adding rice and cooked chicken makes it filling enough for an evening meal

1 tbsp olive oil
1 onion, finely sliced
1 red chilli, finely chopped
20g lemon grass paste
150g easy cook white rice
400ml reduced-fat coconut milk
1.2 litres chicken stock, hot
2 tsp fish sauce
251g pack diced chicken by Sainsbury's
5 spring onions, trimmed
and thinly sliced

150g mange tout, trimmed
and cut into thin strips
1 lime, halved (one half cut into
small wedges)
1/4 x 31g pack fresh coriander
by Sainsbury's, leaves picked
1/4 x 28g pack fresh mint by Sainsbury's,
leaves picked

1 Heat the oil in a large flameproof pan, add the onion and cook for 5 mins. Stir through the chilli and lemon grass paste, and cook for a further 1 min.

2 Add the rice and pour in the coconut milk, stock, fish sauce and diced chicken. Simmer for 15 mins.

3 Add the spring onions and mange tout, then bring to the boil and simmer for 5 mins until heated through.

4 Squeeze the lime half into the soup, then stir through half of the fresh herbs. Divide the soup between 4 bowls, scatter over the remaining herbs and garnish with a lime wedge to serve.

Per serving: 387 cals, 14g fat, 10g sat fat, 5.9g total sugars, 1.6g salt

Cook's tip
Make this vegetarian by leaving out the chicken and adding in red pepper strips and some green cabbage with the mange tout.

A rich and creamy chicken soup with a subtle hint of spice

Serves 4
Prep time: 15 mins
Cook time: 30 mins

Ready in 45 mins

Broccoli & Stilton soup

Two classic flavours combine in this soup, served with cheesy toasts

---

1 tbsp olive oil
5 spring onions, trimmed and chopped
3 cloves garlic, chopped
2-3 sprigs fresh thyme, leaves picked
2 medium floury potatoes, peeled and diced into 1-2cm cubes

500g broccoli (about 2 small heads), roughly chopped, including stalks
75g blue Stilton, crumbled
1.5 litres vegetable stock, hot
½ white baguette, sliced into 8
30g mature British Cheddar, grated

---

1 Heat the olive oil in a large saucepan over a medium heat. Add the spring onions and garlic and cook for 3-4 mins.

2 Turn up the heat and add most of the thyme and potato. Cook for 3-4 mins, gently stirring until the ingredients are combined. Stir through the broccoli and Stilton and pour over the stock. Bring to the boil then reduce the heat, cover and simmer for 20 mins, until the potatoes are completely soft.

3 Pour into a blender or using a hand held blender, purée until smooth. Season with salt and freshly ground black pepper.

4 Meanwhile, preheat the grill to medium-high. Just before you're ready to serve the soup, sprinkle the baguette slices with the Cheddar and grill for 1-2 mins until golden. Garnish with the remaining thyme leaves. Ladle the soup into bowls and top with the baguette slices.

Per serving: 384 cals, 14g fat, 7.1g sat fat, 3.6g total sugars, 2.1g salt

Serves 4
Prep time: 10 mins
Cook time: 40 mins

Ready in 50 mins

Chunky tomato & lentil soup

A lightly spiced, flavoursome soup that's delicious served with naan bread

2 tbsp olive oil
1 onion, finely chopped
3-4cm piece of fresh ginger, peeled
and finely chopped
3 cloves garlic, finely sliced
1 tsp ground cumin
2 tsp garam masala

1 red pepper, deseeded and finely chopped
500g passata
250g dried red lentils, washed thoroughly
1.2 litres vegetable stock, hot
50ml single cream
260g pack plain naans by Sainsbury's,
cooked to pack instructions and halved

1 Heat the olive oil in a large saucepan over a medium heat. Add the onion and fry for 4-5 mins until soft. Add the ginger, garlic, ground cumin and garam masala, and stir. Add the red pepper and cook for another 3-4 mins.

2 Pour in the passata, lentils and stock and stir well. Bring to a boil, then reduce the heat and simmer for 20-25 mins or until the lentils are soft.

3 Season with salt and freshly ground black pepper, keeping the soup over a low heat. Serve with a drizzle of cream and the warm naan.

Per serving: 427 cals, 16g fat, 5.6g sat fat, 13g total sugars, 2.1g salt

Leek, haddock & potato soup

Heat 1 tbsp olive oil in a pan and cook 1 chopped onion and 2 sliced leeks for 10 mins over a low heat. Stir in the chopped stalks from a 28g pack parsley and 400g peeled and diced potatoes. Cook for 5 mins, then add 250ml semi-skimmed milk and 700ml vegetable stock. Bring to the boil, then simmer for 15 mins. Season. Purée half of the soup, then return to the pan with 300g skinless and boneless haddock, chopped, and cook for 5 mins. Garnish with the parsley leaves and lemon wedges to serve.

Serves 4 Ready: 45 mins Prep time: 5 mins Cook time: 40 mins
Per serving: 253 cals, 5.4g fat, 1.6g sat fat, 8.1g total sugars, 1.2g salt

Serves 4
Prep time: 15 mins
Cook time: 35 mins

Ready in 50 mins

Moroccan-style chicken soup

Harissa and dried apricots give this soup a delicious spicy sweetness, while the chickpeas and barley turn it into a satisfying meal

1 tbsp rapeseed or vegetable oil
1 onion, chopped
2 carrots, peeled and chopped
1 clove garlic, chopped
3 tsp harissa spices by Sainsbury's
125g pearl barley
2 x 390g cartons Italian chopped tomatoes with basil, chilli & oregano by Sainsbury's

410g tin chickpeas by Sainsbury's, drained and rinsed
50g dried apricots, chopped
251g pack diced chicken by Sainsbury's
½ x 28g pack fresh flat-leaf parsley by Sainsbury's, chopped, plus extra to garnish
Lemon wedges, to serve

1 Heat the oil in a large saucepan, add the onion and carrots cook for 5 mins. Stir in the garlic and harissa, and cook for a further 1 min.

2 Add the pearl barley, tomatoes and 1.3 litres water. Bring to the boil, then simmer for 15 mins.

3 Stir in the chickpeas, apricots, chicken and parsley. Cook for 10 mins or until the chicken is cooked through with no pink remaining. Season with salt and freshly ground black pepper, garnish with the extra parsley and serve with the lemon wedges.

Per serving: 335 cals, 6.2g fat, 0.8g sat fat, 19g total sugars, 0.9g salt

Cook's tip
This is perfect for freezing. Cool at room temperature, then freeze in a plastic container with a tight-fitting lid, allowing enough space for expansion, for up to 3 months. Defrost in the fridge overnight and reheat until piping hot throughout.

A warming and delicately spiced meal in a bowl

Serves 4
Prep time: 15 mins
Cook time: 35 mins

Ready in 50 mins

Bouillabaisse-style fish & tomato soup

This easy version of a French classic makes a hearty, flavour-packed meal

2 tbsp olive oil
1 onion, finely chopped
3 cloves garlic, roughly chopped
½ bulb of fennel, roughly chopped
1 red pepper, deseeded and thinly sliced
Zest of 1 orange
Pinch of saffron strands
390g carton Italian chopped tomatoes in tomato juice by Sainsbury's

750ml fish stock, hot
500g fresh mussels, see cook's tip, below
260g pack skinless and boneless cod fillet by Sainsbury's, cut into 2-3cm chunks
180g raw king prawns
4 tbsp roughly chopped flat-leaf parsley
1 white baguette, roughly torn

1   Heat the olive oil in a large, deep pan over medium-high heat. Add the onion, garlic, fennel and red pepper and cook for 5-6 mins, until just beginning to soften.

2   Add the orange zest, saffron, tomatoes, and fish stock, and gently stir to combine. Bring the soup to a simmer and cook for about 20 mins until the vegetables are tender and the liquid has reduced by a third.

3   Reduce the heat to medium, add the mussels, cover and cook for 3 mins, before adding the fish and prawns. Cover and cook for about 2-3 mins more, until the fish has just turned opaque and the prawns have become firm and pink. Don't cook the fish for any longer than needed.

4   Serve straightaway, sprinkled with the parsley and topped with the torn crusty bread.

Per serving: 468 cals, 8.5g fat, 1.8g sat fat, 9.8g total sugars, 3.7g salt

Cook's tip
To prepare the mussels, remove the beards and scrub clean. Discard any with cracked shells or that don't close when tapped on a work surface. After cooking, discard any that haven't opened.

Serves 4
Prep time: 15 mins
Cook time: 2 hours

Ready in 2 hours 15 mins

Goulash soup

No chapter on one-pot soups would be complete without this classic hearty Hungarian soup! Enjoy with crusty bread for a filling winter supper

---

2 tbsp olive oil
457g pack British lean casserole steak by Sainsbury's, cut into 2.5cm cubes
1 onion, finely chopped
2 celery sticks, trimmed and roughly chopped
1 red pepper, deseeded and chopped
2 carrots, peeled and finely diced
2 bay leaves
2 tsp paprika

1 tsp cayenne pepper
390g carton Italian chopped tomatoes in tomato juice by Sainsbury's
1 litre beef stock, hot
2 medium floury potatoes, cut into 2cm cubes
250g cooked beetroot by Sainsbury's, cut into 2cm dice
4 tbsp soured cream
1 tbsp fresh parsley, roughly chopped

---

1 Heat 1 tbsp olive oil in a large flameproof casserole over a high heat. Add the beef cubes and fry, in batches, until brown and caramelised. Set aside.

2 Reduce the heat to low and add the remaining olive oil to the pan with the onion, celery, red pepper and carrots. Gently fry for 5-6 mins until just starting to soften. Add the bay leaves, sprinkle over the paprika and cayenne and fry for a further 1-2 mins.

3 Return the beef to the pan with the chopped tomatoes and beef stock. Increase the heat to medium, then cover and simmer for 1 hour.

4 Remove the lid and stir through the potatoes and beetroot. Simmer, uncovered, for the final 45 mins or until the potatoes are tender.

5 Serve in bowls garnished with soured cream and parsley.

Per serving: 578 cals, 29g fat, 12g sat fat, 15g total sugars, 1.6g salt

poultry

Serves 4
Prep time: 10 mins
Cook time: 15 mins

1 of 5
A-DAY

Ready in 25 mins

Chicken chow mein

Get the wok (or frying pan) hot and throw in these ingredients for a Chinese-style stir fry that's ready in a flash

½ tbsp olive oil
333g pack British chicken breast fillets by Sainsbury's, cut into bite-size pieces
2 tsp ginger paste
2 tsp garlic purée
410g pack free range fresh egg noodles by Sainsbury's (ready to cook)
1 tbsp sesame oil

175g pack babycorn & mange tout by Sainsbury's, halved lengthways
1 red pepper, deseeded and sliced
5 spring onions, trimmed and finely sliced
175ml pouch Chinese stir fry sauce by Sainsbury's

1 Heat the olive oil in a wok, add the chicken and stir fry until browned all over. Add the ginger and garlic and cook for another 3-4 mins.

2 Meanwhile, pierce the bag of noodles with a fork and cook in the microwave for 2-3 mins, then toss in the sesame oil.

3 Add the babycorn and mange tout, red pepper and half the spring onions to the wok. Stir fry for 2-3 mins. Add the noodles and sauce and toss together. Cook for 2 mins, until the chicken is cooked through and no pink colour remains. Garnish with the remaining spring onions.

Per serving: 417 cals, 14g fat, 1.9g sat fat, 8g total sugars, 1.2g salt

Coronation chicken

Heat 1 tbsp olive oil in a saucepan and cook 1 chopped onion for 5 mins until soft. Stir in 1 tbsp each korma curry paste and tomato purée and cook for 2 mins. Remove from the heat and stir in 2 tbsp mango chutney, 100g sultanas, 200ml half-fat créme fraîche and 100ml low-fat natural yogurt. Fold in 500g cooked leftover chicken, torn into chunks. Top with toasted flaked almonds and serve with 100g bag watercress, spinach and rocket salad by Sainsbury's and some crusty bread.

Serves 4 Ready: 17 mins Prep time: 5-10 mins Cook time: 7 mins

Per serving: 544 cals, 16g fat, 6.5g sat fat, 31g total sugars, 1.5g salt

Serves 4
Prep time: 10 mins
Cook time: 30 mins

Ready in 40 mins

Chunky turkey & veg nachos

Forget takeaways - here's an easy Friday night treat the kids will love. Turkey mince makes a delicious alternative to the usual beef

1 tbsp olive oil
1 red onion, finely chopped
500g pack lean British turkey thigh mince by Sainsbury's
2 courgettes, trimmed and finely chopped
420g tin mixed beans in mild chilli sauce by Sainsbury's

390g carton Italian chopped tomatoes with basil, chilli & oregano by Sainsbury's
200g pack basics tortilla chips
50g mature Cheddar, grated
5 spring onions, trimmed and thinly sliced

1 Heat the oil in a large saucepan. Add the onion and cook for 5 mins until soft. Add the turkey mince and brown for 5 mins, breaking it up with a wooden spoon as it cooks. Add the courgettes and cook for 2 mins.

2 Add the mixed beans and chopped tomatoes and bring to a simmer. Reduce the heat, cover and cook gently for 15 mins, stirring occasionally. Season with salt and freshly ground black pepper.

3 Put the tortilla chips on a large serving platter (or divide between 4 plates), spoon over the chilli, then scatter over the Cheddar and spring onions. Serve immediately.

Per serving: 657 cals, 26.2g fat, 5g sat fat, 13.1g total sugars, 2.2g salt

Cook's tip
Make your food go further by adding 500g chopped mushrooms with the courgettes, and using an extra carton of chopped tomatoes. This will make enough chilli for two meals. You can freeze the extra batch for up to 1 month: just defrost overnight in the fridge before reheating until piping hot.

Serves 4
Prep time: 10 mins
Cook time: 35 mins

Ready in 45 mins

Chicken biryani

Simple, all-in-one suppers don't get much tastier than this easy Indian-inspired dish that's bursting with fragrant spices

1½ tbsp olive oil

400g pack British mini chicken fillets by Sainsbury's, cut into chunks

1 onion, finely sliced

2 cloves garlic, sliced

3 tbsp balti curry paste

300g basmati rice

2 dried bay leaves

1 cinnamon stick

6 cardamom pods

700ml chicken stock, hot

100g frozen peas

½ x 31g pack fresh coriander by Sainsbury's, roughly chopped

Juice of 1 lemon

20g toasted flaked almonds

1 Preheat the oven to 200ºC, fan 180ºC, gas 6. Heat half the oil in a flameproof casserole on the hob and cook the chicken for 5 mins until browned. Transfer to a bowl and set aside.

2 In the same casserole, add the remaining oil and the onion, and cook for 5 mins until golden, adding a splash of water if needed. Stir in the garlic and curry paste, and cook for 30 seconds before adding the rice, bay leaves, cinnamon stick, cardamom pods and browned chicken. Stir to coat the chicken and rice all over.

3 Add in the hot stock, scraping up any of the bits from the bottom of the pan. Bring to a simmer. Cover with foil followed by a tight-fitting lid and place in the oven to cook for 15 mins.

4 Remove from the oven, stir through the peas, then return to the oven for a further 5 mins, until the rice is tender.

5 Stir in the chopped coriander and lemon juice, and scatter with the flaked almonds to serve.

Per serving: 551 cals, 12.4g fat, 1.8g sat fat, 4.2g total sugars, 0.54g salt

Curry and rice in one pot makes this dish so easy

Ready in 55 mins

Chicken & tarragon pie

Serves 6
Prep time: 15 mins
Cook time: 40 mins

The golden pastry top makes this simple pie look so appetising. Leeks, peas and tarragon add lots of fresh flavour to the chicken filling

2 tbsp olive oil

600g chicken thigh fillets, chopped

1 onion, finely chopped

3 leeks, trimmed and sliced

3 cloves garlic, finely chopped

150ml white wine

2 tbsp plain flour, mixed with 2 tbsp water to form a paste

400ml chicken stock, hot

1 tsp Dijon mustard

200g frozen garden peas

½ x 20g pack fresh tarragon by Sainsbury's, leaves picked and chopped

375g pack ready-rolled light puff pastry by Sainsbury's

1 medium egg, beaten

1 Heat 1 tbsp olive oil in a large, shallow flameproof casserole and cook the chicken for 5 mins until golden. Remove from the pan and set aside.

2 Preheat the oven to 200°C, fan 180°C, gas 6. Meanwhile, heat the remaining olive oil in the casserole over a medium heat and cook the onion and leeks for 10 mins, stirring in the garlic for the last 1 min.

3 Pour in the white wine, bring to the boil and simmer for 3 mins before stirring in the flour mixture and stock. Bring to the boil and stir in the cooked chicken and Dijon mustard. Cook for 5 mins, then stir in the peas and tarragon, and season with salt and freshly ground black pepper.

4 Meanwhile, lay the pastry out on a floured surface. Using a 10cm round cutter, cut out 9 circles. Brush each circle on one side with the egg, then lay 8 circles onto the pie, around the sides, slightly overlapping, and put the remaining circle in the middle. Brush again with the egg and cook in the oven for 15 mins, until the pastry is golden.

Per serving: 656 cals, 33g fat, 10g sat fat, 7.8g total sugars, 1.7g salt

Serves 4
Prep time: 10 mins
Cook time: 45 mins

Ready in 55 mins

Chicken & chorizo paella

An impressive dish that will have you dreaming of sunny Spain. Don't leave out the saffron – even though it's just a pinch, it adds that authentic flavour!

1 tbsp olive oil
400g pack diced British chicken breast by Sainsbury's
½ x 225g spicy and smoky chorizo ring by Sainsbury's, sliced on the diagonal
1 onion, chopped
1 clove garlic, chopped

1 tsp paprika
250g Sainsbury's Spanish paella rice
Pinch of saffron strands
1 litre chicken stock, hot
200g frozen peas
1 tbsp chopped fresh parsley

1 Heat ½ tbsp olive oil in a large frying pan over a medium heat. Add the chicken and cook for 10 mins until golden and cooked through, and no pink remains. Stir through the chorizo for the final 2 mins of the cooking time. Remove the chicken and chorizo from the pan and set aside.

2 Heat the remaining olive oil in the pan, add the onion and cook for 5-10 mins until soft. Add the garlic and paprika for the last 1 min.

3 Stir through the paella rice, then add the saffron strands and stock. Bring to the boil, then reduce to a simmer and cook, covered, for 25 mins. Stir in the peas during the final 2 mins of cooking.

4 Stir the chicken and chorizo through the rice mixture, along with half the parsley. Serve in warm bowls garnished with the remaining parsley.

Per serving: 581 cals, 18g fat, 6.1g sat fat, 4g total sugars, 1.9g salt

Fragrant and spicy, this is a taste of sunny Spain

Serves 4
Prep time: 15 mins
Cook time: 35-40 mins

Ready in 55 mins

Mediterranean chicken

This light chicken stew makes a great dish for al fresco entertaining. Olives, rosemary and white wine give it plenty of punchy flavour

2 tbsp olive oil
460g pack skinless, boneless British chicken thighs by Sainsbury's, cut into chunks
1 onion, sliced
2 cloves garlic, finely chopped
100ml white wine
390g carton Italian chopped tomatoes in tomato juice by Sainsbury's

100g pitted kalamata olives, drained
50g sultanas
2 sprigs rosemary, leaves picked and chopped
2 x 250g packs microwaveable basmati rice by Sainsbury's
260g bag young spinach by Sainsbury's

1 Heat the oil in a large, heavy-based pan. Add the chicken, in batches, and fry over a high heat for 5 mins until browned. Add the onion and reduce the heat to medium, cook for 5 mins, then stir in the garlic.

2 Turn up the heat, add the wine and boil for 1 min. Add the tomatoes, olives, sultanas and rosemary, then simmer gently for 20 mins until the sauce thickens slightly.

3 Meanwhile, cook the rice according to pack instructions in the microwave. Stir the fresh spinach into the chicken mixture, leave to wilt for 1 min, then serve with the rice.

Per serving: 597 cals, 27g fat, 5.5g sat fat, 14g total sugars, 1.2g salt

Cook's tip
This dish is perfect for using up roast leftovers.
Cook the onion and garlic without the chicken
in step 1, then add your leftover chicken with
the tomatoes in step 2.

An easy dish that's full of flavour and colour

Serves 4
Prep time: 15 mins
Cook time: 45 mins

Ready in 1 hour

Curried chicken pie

Topped with filo rather than puff pastry, this crunchy pie is easy to make and is a healthier alternative to traditional pies

30g unsalted butter
1 onion, finely chopped
1 tbsp medium curry powder
460g pack British chicken breast fillets by Sainsbury's, diced
40g plain flour
400ml semi-skimmed milk

300g broccoli, trimmed and cut into small florets
1 tbsp rapeseed or vegetable oil
2 sheets filo pastry
2 x 200g packs Chantenay carrots & fine beans by Sainsbury's

1 Preheat the oven to 200°C, fan 180°C, gas 6. Put the butter in a shallow flameproof casserole over a medium heat, add the onion and cook for 5 mins until soft. Add the curry powder and cook for a further 1 min, until fragrant. Add the chicken and cook for 5 mins, until golden and nearly cooked through.

2 Stir in the flour and cook for a further 2 mins, then remove from the heat and gradually stir in the milk. Return to the heat, stirring continuously to prevent lumps forming, until the mixture thickens.

3 When the sauce comes to the boil, reduce the heat and simmer for 5 mins. Add the broccoli and season with salt and freshly ground black pepper.

4 Brush the rapeseed oil onto one side of each filo sheet. Gently scrunch up the pastry and arrange on top of the pie to cover the filling. Lightly brush with the remaining oil and bake for 20 mins, until golden and crisp on top.

5 Just before the end of the cooking time, put the carrots and beans into a microwave-proof bowl with 1 tbsp water, cover with cling film and cook on high for 3-4 mins. Season with salt and freshly ground black pepper and serve with the pie.

Per serving: 466 cals, 14.7g fat, 6.5g sat fat, 13.7g total sugars, 1.74g salt

Serves 4
Prep time: 10 mins
Cook time: 55 mins

Ready in 1 hour 5 mins

Baked chicken with butternut squash

This dish has a mouthwatering combination of seasonal flavours - the butternut squash caramelises, giving it a nutty sweetness

850g pack British chicken thighs & drumsticks by Sainsbury's
200g shallots, peeled and halved
750g baby potatoes, cut into thick wedges
400g butternut squash, peeled, deseeded and cut into wedges
4 cloves garlic, unpeeled

1 tbsp olive oil
30g walnut halves
15g pack fresh thyme by Sainsbury's, leaves picked, with a few sprigs left whole to garnish
50g Abergavenny goats' cheese by Sainsbury's, crumbled

1 Preheat the oven to 200°C, fan 180°C, gas 6. Put the chicken in a large baking dish with the shallots, potatoes, butternut squash and garlic. Drizzle with the oil and toss the veg and chicken to coat. Season with salt and freshly ground black pepper, and roast in the oven for 45 mins, turning the veg and chicken halfway through.

2 Remove the tray from the oven and stir through the walnuts and the thyme leaves. Roast for a further 10 mins until the chicken is cooked through (with no pink meat remaining), the skin is crispy, the vegetables are tender and the walnuts are toasted.

3 To serve, scatter over the crumbled goats' cheese and garnish with the thyme sprigs.

Per serving: 481 cals, 20g fat, 5.3g sat fat, 8.1g total sugars, 0.36g salt

Cook's tip
Why not experiment with this recipe and try different veg – sweet potato works well instead of squash – or try adding a few wedges of fennel, too.

Serves 4
Prep time: 15 mins
Cook time: 1 hour
15 mins

Ready in 1 hour 30 mins

Chicken, leek & barley hotpot

Tarragon adds a distinctive tang to this sweet and creamy chicken dish. You can also make this dish using leftover roast chicken

2 tbsp olive oil	500ml chicken stock, hot
2 cloves garlic, chopped	400g pack diced British chicken breast
1 onion, sliced	by Sainsbury's, cut into chunks
3 carrots, peeled and thickly sliced	4 tbsp double cream
2 leeks, trimmed and sliced	2 tsp wholegrain mustard
100g pearl barley, rinsed well	½ x 20g pack fresh tarragon by Sainsbury's

1 Heat the oil in a large, heavy-based saucepan. Add the garlic, onion, carrots and leeks, cover and cook gently for 10 mins.

2 Pour in the pearl barley and stock, bring to the boil and cook for 1 hour, then add the chicken for the last 10 mins.

3 Stir in the cream, mustard and half of the tarragon. Cook for 5 mins or until the chicken is cooked through with no pink meat remaining, then season with salt and freshly ground black pepper. Sprinkle over the remaining tarragon to serve.

Per serving: 364 cals, 15g fat, 6.2g sat fat, 10g total sugars, 1.3g salt

Cook's tip
This dish is great for using up root veg – simply swap the carrots for any root veg you fancy. Try parsnips, swede, turnips or even a combination of all three (you'll need approx 300g in total).

Serves 4
Prep time: 10 mins
Cook time: 1 hour
10 mins, plus resting

 2 of 5 A-DAY

Ready in 1 hour 35 mins

Chipotle chicken

A twist on a classic roast, the chipotle paste and red pepper purée coating gives this plenty of spicy, smoky flavour. The veg cook in their own foil tray

1.4kg British whole chicken by Sainsbury's
2 unwaxed lemons, quartered
15g pack fresh thyme by Sainsbury's
1 tsp chipotle chilli paste by Sainsbury's
2 tbsp chargrilled red pepper

paste by Sainsbury's
750g baby potatoes, larger ones halved
2 x 400g packs ready to roast
Mediterranean vegetables by Sainsbury's

1 Preheat the oven to 180°C, fan 160°C, gas 4. Stuff the chicken cavity with one of the lemons and half of the thyme. Put the chicken into a large roasting tin, breast side up.

2 Mix the chilli paste with the red pepper paste and spread over the chicken with a knife. Roast on the middle shelf of the oven for 1 hour 10 mins.

3 Add the remaining lemon and the potatoes to the tin 30 mins before the end of the cooking time. At the same time, top the Mediterranean veg with the remaining thyme and put the trays in the oven to cook.

4 At the end of the cooking time, check the chicken is cooked through with no pink meat remaining and clear juices. Remove the chicken from the tin and rest for 15 mins before serving with the veg.

Per serving: 559 cals, 20g fat, 4.5g sat fat, 13g total sugars, 0.59g salt

Couscous chicken salad

Thinly slice 2 courgettes and lightly grill on a griddle pan for 3-4 mins. Put 250g couscous in a bowl. Pour over 300ml boiling water. Cover with cling film and let it sit for 10 mins, then fluff up with a fork, and stir through 300g torn cooked chicken breast, 100g crumbled feta, the zest and juice of 1 lemon and 1 tbsp each chopped fresh chives and parsley.

Serves 4 Ready: 10 mins Prep time: 5 mins Cook time: 5 mins

Per serving: 404 cals, 7.6g fat, 4.8g sat fat, 1.7g total sugars, 0.98g salt

Ready in 1 hour 40 mins

Coq au vin

Serves 4
Prep time: 20 mins
Cook time: 1 hour
20 mins

A classic French one-pot dish that makes a welcoming dinner on a wintry evening. Don't skimp on the red wine – it adds a real depth of flavour

2 tbsp olive oil
850g pack British chicken thighs and drumsticks by Sainsbury's
250g pack smoked bacon lardons by Sainsbury's
200g shallots, peeled but left whole
250g pack closed cup chestnut mushrooms by Sainsbury's, quartered
3 celery sticks, trimmed and chopped

3 cloves garlic, sliced
2 tbsp plain flour
2 bay leaves
2-3 sprigs fresh thyme
500ml red wine
2 x 400g packs ready mashed potato by Sainsbury's
2 tbsp chopped fresh parsley

1 Heat 1 tbsp olive oil in an flameproof casserole over a medium heat and cook the chicken for 5 mins, until golden. You may need to do this in batches to prevent the pan becoming overcrowded. As each batch is done, remove from the casserole and set aside.

2 If you need to, pour a little more oil into the pan and cook the lardons, for 5 mins, until they begin to crisp. Set the lardons aside with the chicken. There will be a lovely sticky layer on the bottom of the pan, which has lots of flavour, so don't be tempted to clean the pot.

3 Add the remaining oil to the pot and cook the whole shallots for 1 min, then add the mushrooms, celery and garlic and cook for 10 mins. Sprinkle over the flour and stir, then return the chicken and bacon to the pan. Add the bay leaves and thyme and pour over the red wine.

4 Bring to the boil, cover and simmer gently for 1 hour until the chicken is cooked through. Season with salt and freshly ground black pepper.

5 Meanwhile, cook the mashed potato according to pack instructions. Garnish the coq au vin with parsley and serve with the mashed potato.

Per serving: 617 cals, 37g fat, 11g sat fat, 4.9g total sugars, 2.8g salt

A delicious French classic that's as popular as ever

Serves 4
Prep time: 15 mins
Cook time: 1 hour 20 mins, plus resting

Ready in 1 hour 50 mins

Italian roast chicken

Roasting a chicken with ratatouille makes a great alternative to a traditional roast - cook it all together in the one baking tin

---

1.35kg British whole chicken by Sainsbury's
2 tbsp olive oil
1 whole bulb of garlic, cut in half horizontally
500g aubergines, cut into 2cm cubes
2 red onions, cut into wedges
1 yellow pepper, deseeded and sliced

2 x 390g cartons Italian chopped tomatoes with olive oil & garlic by Sainsbury's
½ x 28g pack fresh basil by Sainsbury's, roughly torn
2 x 400g pack ready mashed potato by Sainsbury's

---

1 Preheat the oven to 190°C, fan 170°C, gas 5. Place the chicken in a large roasting tin and rub with the oil. Season with salt and freshly ground black pepper, then put the garlic inside the cavity. Roast for 20 mins, then scatter the aubergines, onions and pepper around the chicken and roast for a further 30 mins.

2 Pour the tomatoes into the vegetables in the roasting tin and stir in half the basil. Cook for a further 30 mins until the chicken is fully cooked through with clear juices and no pink colour remaining. Rest for 15 mins.

3 Meanwhile, cook the mash to pack instructions. Slice and serve the chicken with the veg and mash, and garnish with the remaining basil.

Per serving: 539 cals, 20g fat, 6g sat fat, 16g total sugars, 0.82g salt

Noodles with roast chicken

Heat 1 tbsp olive oil in a wok, then add 1 deseeded and sliced red chilli, 1 chopped garlic clove and a knob of ginger, grated. Cook for 1 min, then add 400g cooked torn chicken, a 175g pack babycorn & mange tout, halved, and 2 tbsp sesame seeds. Cook for 2-3 mins, then add a 410g pack free-range egg noodles by Sainsbury's with 1 tbsp sesame oil and 1 tbsp light soy sauce. Stir fry for 3-4 mins, then stir through a 75g bag watercress to serve.

Serves 4 Ready: 15 mins Prep time: 5 mins Cook time: 10 mins

Per serving: 431 cals, 18g fat, 3.5g sat fat, 2.4g total sugars, 0.72g salt

Serves 4
Prep time: 15 mins
Cook time: 2 hours

3 of 5 A-DAY

Ready in 2 hours 15 mins

Braised duck legs with red cabbage

Shallots, star anise and a dash of orange juice create lots of lovely flavours in this dish - a great choice for easy entertaining

1 tbsp vegetable oil

4 duck legs

400g shallots, peeled

2 carrots, peeled and diced

1 celery stick, trimmed and diced

3 cloves garlic, crushed

1 star anise

¼ x 28g pack fresh thyme by Sainsbury's, plus a few extra leaves to garnish

1 red cabbage, chopped

250ml red wine

3 tbsp balsamic vinegar

Zest and juice of 1 orange

300ml chicken stock, hot

2 x 400g packs ready mashed potato by Sainsbury's

1 Preheat the oven to 200°C, fan 180°C, gas 6. On the hob, heat the oil in a shallow flameproof casserole and cook the duck legs for 5 mins each side, until browned, with some of the fat released. Remove the duck legs from the casserole and pour out all but 1 tbsp of the fat.

2 Stir in the shallots, carrots, celery, garlic, star anise and half the thyme, and cook for 10 mins. Stir in the cabbage and cook for a further 5 mins before pouring in the wine, balsamic vinegar, orange zest and juice, and chicken stock. Bring to the boil, then place the duck legs on top, cover and cook for 1 hour in the oven.

3 Reduce the oven temperature to 180°C, fan 160°C, gas 4. Remove the lid from the casserole and cook for a further 30 mins until the meat from the duck is almost falling off the bone.

4 Meanwhile, cook the mashed potato according to pack instructions. Serve with the duck, sprinkled with the reserved thyme and any juices left in the pan drizzled over.

Per serving: 578 cals, 37g fat, 12g sat fat, 16g total sugars, 1.8g salt

meat

Serves 4
Prep time: 5 mins
Cook time: 20 mins

Ready in 25 mins

Pan-fried steak with green cabbage

A very quick dish that's a different way to serve steak. The nigella seeds add a hint of smoky, peppery flavour, and look appetising, too

4 rump steaks
2 tbsp olive oil
6 shallots, peeled and sliced
1 red chilli, deseeded and finely chopped
1 clove garlic, finely chopped
1/2 tsp nigella seeds
100ml brandy

100ml beef stock, hot
1 small sweetheart green cabbage
(about 300g), sliced
1/4 x 31g pack fresh coriander
by Sainsburys, chopped
1/2 white baguette, to serve

1 Heat a large frying pan over a high heat. Rub the steaks with 1 tbsp of the olive oil and season with salt and freshly ground black pepper. Cook the steaks for 3 mins on each side, then remove from the pan and set aside to rest for 6 mins.

2 Meanwhile, add the remaining oil, shallots, chilli, garlic and nigella seeds to the pan and cook for 2 mins, before pouring in the brandy and stock. Bring to the boil and simmer for 3 mins, before stirring in the cabbage and coriander. Cover and allow to steam for 3 mins, then add the steaks back into the pan and baste with the juices.

3 Serve with crusty bread for a quick and easy meal.

Per serving: 634 cals, 31g fat, 12g sat fat, 4.7g total sugars, 1.8g salt

Serves 4
Prep time: 5 mins
Cook time: 25 mins

Ready in 30 mins

Chorizo, tomato & rosemary pasta

The chorizo sausages in this dish give it plenty of smoky flavour.
To spice things up, a pinch of chilli is added – use more if you like it hot!

1 tbsp olive oil
250g pack mini chorizo for cooking
by Sainsbury's, sliced
1 onion, halved and sliced
1 yellow pepper, deseeded and sliced
Pinch of chilli flakes
4 sprigs rosemary, leaves picked and
chopped, plus a few sprigs to garnish

390g carton Italian chopped tomatoes
in tomato juice by Sainsbury's
400ml chicken stock, hot
200g farfalle pasta
200g bag baby leaf spinach by Sainsbury's

1 Heat the oil in a large pan and cook the chorizo slices for 3-4 mins until
golden. Remove from the pan and set aside.

2 Cook the onion, pepper, chilli flakes and rosemary together for 5 mins,
then stir in the chopped tomatoes and the chicken stock. Bring to the boil,
then add the pasta. Cover and cook for 10-12 mins.

3 Remove the lid and return the chorizo to the pan. Stir through the spinach
and let it wilt for 1 min before serving.

Per serving: 554 cals, 29g fat, 9.4g sat fat, 11g total sugars, 3.8g salt

Cook's tip
Traditional products with extra ingredients are
great for one-pot cooking. Try Italian chopped
tomatoes with sliced olives by Sainsbury's in
this dish for an added Mediterranean flavour.

Serves 4
Prep time: 15 mins
Cook time: 20 mins

Ready in 35 mins

Caribbean pork stew

With plenty of colourful veg, this spicy little number looks every bit as good as it tastes. The coconut milk gives the sauce a velvety richness

1 tbsp vegetable oil
460g pack diced British pork leg
by Sainsbury's
2 red onions, cut into wedges
2 tbsp spicy jerk paste by Sainsbury's
1 pack Sainsbury's 3 mixed peppers,
deseeded and sliced
2 carrots, peeled and cut into ribbons using
a vegetable peeler

200ml reduced-fat coconut milk
390g carton Italian chopped tomatoes
in tomato juice by Sainsbury's
100g bag baby leaf spinach by Sainsbury's
½ x 28g pack fresh flat-leaf parsley
by Sainsbury's, roughly chopped
2 x 250g packs microwave long grain rice
by Sainsbury's

1 Heat the oil in a large wok or frying pan. Add the pork and onions and cook for 5 mins until golden and softened. Stir in the jerk paste, peppers and carrots and cook for 10 mins.

2 Stir in the coconut milk and tomatoes, then bring to a simmer and cook for 5 mins, stirring in the spinach and half the parsley for the last min.

3 Meanwhile, cook the rice according to pack instructions. Stir the remaining parsley through the rice and serve with the stew.

Per serving: 500 cals, 15g fat, 6.5g sat fat, 17g total sugars, 1.1g salt

Creamy pork & courgette pasta

Cook 300g fettuccine in a pan of boiling water for 10 mins, then drain, reserving 100ml of the water. Return the pasta to the pan, add 1 tbsp olive oil and 1 chopped clove garlic, and cook for 1 min. Add 300g chopped leftover roast pork and 200g courgettes, peeled into ribbons. Season and mix well. In a small bowl, whisk 2 egg yolks with 75ml single cream and 25g parmesan, then stir it through the pasta, adding the reserved water. Cook over a low heat until the sauce has thickened and the pork is warmed through.

Serves 4 Ready: 20 mins Prep time: 5 mins Cook time: 15 mins

Per serving: 527 cals, 17g fat, 6.6g sat fat, 4.2g total sugars, 0.44g salt

Spicy and colourful — this is a real crowd-pleaser

Serves 4
Prep time: 10 mins
Cook time: 30 mins

 3 of 5 A-DAY

Ready in 40 mins

Sweet potato, bacon & chickpea hash

You won't be able to resist our cover recipe – sweet potato, crispy bacon and baked eggs with a hint of spice. Fantastic for lunch or dinner

2 tbsp olive oil

600g sweet potatoes, scrubbed and cut into bite-size chunks

300g pack smoked back bacon rashers by Sainsbury's, roughly chopped

1 onion, finely chopped

1 clove garlic, crushed

1 tsp mild chilli powder

410g tin chickpeas by Sainsbury's, drained and rinsed

2 tbsp double concentrate tomato purée by Sainsbury's

100g bag baby leaf spinach by Sainsbury's

4 medium eggs

1 red chilli, deseeded and finely sliced

1 Preheat the oven to 180ºC, fan 160ºC, gas 4. Heat 1 tbsp of the oil in a large, ovenproof frying pan or dish over a medium heat. Add the sweet potato chunks and cook, covered, for 5 mins. Turn the heat up to high and add the bacon. Stir briskly until the bacon is crisp.

2 Reduce the heat, add the remaining oil and stir in the onion, garlic and chilli powder. Cook for 5 mins, until the onion is soft, then stir in the chickpeas, tomato purée and mix well. Season with salt and freshly ground black pepper, then add the spinach and stir until wilted.

3 Make four deep indents in the top of the mixture and break an egg into each. Bake in the oven for 10 mins, until the egg is set to your liking. Top with a few slices of red chilli, if you like, to serve.

Per serving: 563 cals, 25g fat, 6.7g sat fat, 13g total sugars, 1.9g salt

So easy, so tasty! A great dish
for lunch or dinner

Serves 4
Prep time: 10 mins
Cook time: 30 mins

Ready in 40 mins

Summer lamb & apricot tagine

A Moroccan-style dish that's fragrant and full of flavour. Serving it with couscous keeps things simple, making it a great option for a midweek dinner

2 tbsp olive oil
411g pack diced lamb by Sainsbury's
1 onion, chopped
2 cloves garlic, chopped
1 tsp ground cinnamon
½ tsp ground ginger
2 x 390g cartons chopped tomatoes in tomato juice by Sainsbury's
400ml chicken stock, hot
1 tbsp clear honey

150g ready-to-eat dried apricots, cut into quarters
410g tin chickpeas by Sainsbury's, drained and rinsed
260g bag young spinach by Sainsbury's
250g couscous
28g pack fresh flat-leaf parsley by Sainsbury's, finely chopped
25g flaked almonds

1 Heat half the oil in a large saucepan and cook the diced lamb for 5 mins, until golden. Remove with a slotted spoon and set aside.

2 Heat the remaining oil and cook the onion for 5-10 mins, adding the garlic and spices for the last 1 min. Pour in the tomatoes and the hot stock. Add the honey and apricots, bring to a simmer and cook for 10 mins.

3 Stir through the chickpeas and lamb, and cook for a further 5 mins, stirring in the spinach for the last 2 mins.

4 Meanwhile, place the couscous in a bowl and pour over 300ml boiling water. Cover the bowl with cling film and let it sit for 10 mins, then remove the cling film and fluff up the grains using a fork. Stir through the chopped parsley and flaked almonds, and serve with the tagine.

Per serving: 799 cals, 27g fat, 7.8g sat fat, 27g total sugars, 1.2g salt

Cook's tip
Don't want to serve this with couscous? Why not add sweet potato or butternut squash cubes with the honey and apricots, and cook as above.

Ready in 45 mins

Pea & bacon risotto

Serves 4
Prep time: 5 mins
Cook time: 40 mins

Risotto is a great one-pot dish that you can add all kinds of ingredients to. This one uses items you may already have in the fridge, so it's a great standby recipe

1 tbsp olive oil
1 onion, chopped
1 clove garlic, finely chopped
200g unsmoked back bacon, fat removed, and roughly chopped
300g arborio rice

1 litre vegetable stock, hot
200g fresh shelled peas
30g parmesan, grated
¼ x 28g pack fresh flat-leaf parsley by Sainsbury's, finely chopped

1 Heat the oil in a large saucepan. Cook the onion and garlic for 5 mins. Add the bacon and cook for 6-8 mins until crisp. Tip in the rice and stir so that it's coated in the oil.

2 Add the stock to the pan, a ladleful at a time, stirring after each addition until the liquid is absorbed. Once the rice is almost cooked (about 20 mins) and the stock almost all absorbed, add the peas with the last ladleful of stock and cook for a further 5 mins. Season with salt and freshly ground black pepper, then stir through 25g of the cheese and top with the parsley, more black pepper and the remaining cheese to serve.

Per serving: 453 cals, 9.9g fat, 3.5g sat fat, 3.6g total sugars, 1.98g salt

Cook's tip
For an alternative take on this recipe, why not swap the parsley for mint and stir through a couple of tablespoons of crème fraîche at the end.

This easy risotto is a great mealtime standby

Serves 4
Prep time: 15 mins
Cook time: 30 mins

Ready in 45 mins

Meatloaf with cherry tomato salad

An American family favourite that's especially popular with kids

500g pack lean beef steak mince by Sainsbury's

1 tsp smoked paprika by Sainsbury's

50g fresh breadcrumbs

50g sage & onion stuffing (from a pack)

1 carrot, peeled and grated

4 large sprigs rosemary, 1 sprig finely chopped and the others left whole

1 ½ tbsp Worcestershire sauce

1 large egg, lightly beaten

2 rashers pancetta, halved

170g bag Italian style baby leaf salad by Sainsbury's

½ x 335g pack Sainsbury's cherry tomatoes, halved

1 Preheat the oven to 180°C, fan 160°C, gas 4. Line the bottom of a 1-litre loaf tin with baking parchment and put a strip of paper across the middle and up over the sides of the tin to make it easier to lift out the meatloaf.

2 For the meatloaf, in a large bowl mix together the mince, paprika, breadcrumbs, sage & onion stuffing granules, carrot, chopped rosemary, Worcestershire sauce and egg. Mix well, and season with salt and freshly ground black pepper. Spoon the mixture into the lined loaf tin, then lay the remaining rosemary sprigs and the halved pancetta slices across the top on the diagonal, leaving a space in between.

3 Put the loaf tin on a baking tray and cook for 30 mins.

4 Remove the meatloaf from the tin and transfer to a board with the pancetta facing up, using the strip of baking parchment to help lift it out. Slice and serve with the salad and cherry tomatoes.

Per serving: 353 cals, 19g fat, 8.2g sat fat, 5.9g total sugars, 0.86g salt

Serves 6
Prep time: 15 mins
Cook time: 35 mins

Ready in 50 mins

Sticky sausages with cider sauce

Maple syrup adds a delicious sticky glaze to the pork sausages, while a dash of cider gives the sauce a burst of appley sweetness

2 x 400g packs Taste the Difference
ultimate outdoor-bred pork sausages
3 apples, cored and quartered
16 shallots, peeled and halved
6 cloves garlic
3 tbsp maple syrup

2 tbsp olive oil
400ml Sainsbury's English vintage cider
3 tbsp crème fraîche
1 tsp Dijon mustard
2 x 400g packs ready mashed potato,
carrot & swede

1 Preheat the oven to 200°C, fan 180°C, gas 6.

2 Place the sausages, apples, shallots and garlic cloves in a roasting tin. Drizzle with the maple syrup and oil, and roast for 25 mins.

3 Remove the sausages, apples, shallots and garlic, and keep warm. Place the roasting tin on the hob and add the cider. Bring to the boil, stirring, until reduced by a quarter. Stir in the crème fraîche and mustard, then season with salt and freshly ground black pepper.

4 Meanwhile, pierce the packs of mash and cook to pack instructions. Serve the sausages, apples and shallots with the root vegetable mash and the sauce poured over.

Per serving: 607 cals, 39g fat, 15g sat fat, 20g total sugars, 2.4g salt

Cook's tip
If you have more time, make your own mash by using 1.25kg potato and/or veg of your choice. Cut into the same size dice and cook for 15-20 mins, then mash with a little butter and milk, season and serve.

Ready in 1 hour

Lamb balti

Serves 4
Prep time: 10 mins
Cook time: 50 mins

The butternut squash adds a lovely rich sweetness to this curry while using a ready-made balti paste will save you plenty of time in the kitchen

1 tbsp vegetable oil
1 red onion, sliced
500g butternut squash, peeled and roughly chopped
2 cloves garlic, chopped
400g lamb leg steak, cut into large pieces
4 tbsp balti paste

390g carton Italian chopped tomatoes in tomato juice by Sainsbury's
500ml chicken stock, hot
200g fine green beans
1/4 x 31g pack fresh coriander by Sainsbury's
4 be good to yourself mini naan breads, heated to pack instructions

1 Heat the oil in a large pan and cook the onion and butternut squash for 10 mins, adding in the garlic for the last 1 min.

2 Add the lamb and fry for 5 mins, then stir in the balti paste for the last 1 min. Pour in the chopped tomatoes and the chicken stock, and bring to the boil. Cook for 25 mins, then add in the beans and cook for a further 5 mins.

3 Stir through half the coriander and season with salt and pepper, then serve with the naan breads and the remaining coriander sprinkled over.

Per serving: 518 cals, 20g fat, 6.5g sat fat, 14g total sugars, 2.0g salt

Jewelled lamb bulgar wheat

Place 100g bulgar wheat in a pan, add 350ml water and cook for 10-15 mins, to pack instructions. Let the bulgar wheat cool for 5 mins, then stir in a 100g pot pomegranate seeds, 100g crumbled feta, 150g leftover roast lamb, 5 chopped spring onions, 1/2 x 250g pack vine-ripened tomatoes, roughly chopped, 1/4 deseeded and chopped cucumber and a small handful each of chopped mint and parsley. Season with salt and freshly ground black pepper, then serve with tzatziki to drizzle over.

Serves 4 Ready: 25 mins Prep time: 10 mins Cook time: 10-15 mins

Per serving: 232 cals, 12g fat, 6.8g sat fat, 5.6g total sugars, 0.85g salt

Serves 4
Prep time: 15 mins
Cook time: 45 mins

Ready in 1 hour

Pork loin with roasted seasonal veg

This summery take on roast pork with mozzarella and pesto gives this dish a delicious Italian twist and makes a great holiday celebration meal

400g pack Taste the Difference pork tenderloin fillet
1 tbsp roasted red pepper pesto
80g drained mozzarella, chopped
70g pack prosciutto crudo slices by Sainsbury's
200g baby Chantenay carrots, scrubbed

300g baby potatoes, larger ones halved
½ x 250g pack cooked beetroot in natural juices by Sainsbury's, drained and cut into wedges
1½ tbsp olive oil
Few sprigs fresh flat-leaf parsley, washed and chopped, to garnish (optional)

1 Preheat the oven to 200°C, fan 180°C, gas 6. Cut the pork tenderloin in half lengthways, but not all the way through. Open out the pork and bash with a rolling pin until slightly flattened.

2 Spread with pesto, then scatter over the mozzarella pieces. Fold the pork over to close. Lay the prosciutto slices side-by-side, overlapping slightly. Place the pork fillet on top and wrap in the prosciutto.

3 Place the pork in the middle of a shallow baking tray, putting the carrots and potatoes on one side and the beetroot on the other. Drizzle the veg with the oil and season with salt and freshly black pepper.

4 Cook in the oven for 45 mins, covering the pork with foil for the final 15 mins of the cooking time. Cut the pork into slices and serve with the veg, the pan juices drizzled over and garnished with the parsley.

Per serving: 424 cals, 20.3g fat, 7.5g sat fat, 5.3g total sugars, 1.31g salt

Cook's tip
You could use green pesto instead of red, or any of the other ready-to-use pastes in the by Sainsbury's range.

Serves 4
Prep time: 10 mins
Cook time: 55 mins

Ready in 1 hour 5 mins

Meatball, lentil & cabbage hotpot

Using ready-made meatballs in this fantastic family-friendly hotpot cuts your prep time to the minimum

1 tbsp rapeseed or vegetable oil
550g pack Just Cook beef meatballs with tomato sauce & parmesan by Sainsbury's
1 onion, finely chopped
1 clove garlic, crushed
1 tsp smoked paprika, plus an extra pinch to garnish
390g carton Italian chopped tomatoes with basil & oregano by Sainsbury's

500ml beef stock, hot
120g dried green lentils
½ x 28g pack fresh flat-leaf parsley by Sainsbury's, chopped, plus extra to garnish
¼ Savoy cabbage, shredded
1 courgette, trimmed, halved horizontally, and cut into crescents
4 tsp half-fat crème fraîche

1 Heat the oil in a large, deep pot over a medium heat. Add the meatballs and cook for 10 mins, turning, until brown all over. Remove them from the pot and set aside.

2 Add the onion, garlic and paprika to the pan and cook for 5 mins, until the onion is soft. Return the meatballs to the pan with the tomatoes, stock, lentils and the sachets of sauce and parmesan from the meatball pack. Turn up the heat and boil for 10 mins. Reduce the heat and simmer, covered, for 20 mins, until the lentils are tender.

3 Stir in the parsley, cabbage and courgette, and cook for a further 10 mins. Serve with a dollop of the crème fraîche, a sprinkling of the extra paprika and a scattering of parsley.

Per serving: 376 cals, 17.9g fat, 5.6g sat fat, 11.7g total sugars, 1.52g salt

Cook's tip
You don't have to use the Just Cook meatballs for this recipe. Any beef or lamb meatballs will work just as well. Why not make your own?

Ready in 1 hour 10 mins

Greek lamb bake

Serves 4
Prep time: 15 mins
Cook time: 55 mins

Feta and oregano give this mouthwatering bake its Mediterranean tang

2 tbsp olive oil

4 lamb leg steaks by Sainsbury's

1 red onion, sliced into thin wedges

1 aubergine, trimmed and chopped
into 2cm cubes

1 courgette, trimmed and chopped into
2cm cubes

3 cloves garlic, roughly chopped

1 tsp cumin seeds

1 tbsp tomato purée

500g baby potatoes, scrubbed and halved

300ml vegetable stock, hot

390g carton Italian chopped tomatoes
in tomato juice by Sainsbury's

100g feta, crumbled

1 tbsp fresh oregano, leaves picked and
roughly chopped

1 Heat 1 tbsp of the olive oil in a large, shallow flameproof casserole over
a high heat. Add the lamb steaks and fry for 2-3 mins on each side until
the meat begins to brown. Set the lamb aside.

2 Preheat the oven to 180°C, fan 160°C, gas 4. Add the remaining olive oil
to the casserole and fry the onion, aubergine, and courgette for 3-4 mins
until they begin to turn golden. Stir through the garlic, cumin seeds and
tomato purée, and cook for a further 2 mins.

3 Add the baby potatoes, vegetable stock and tomatoes to the pot and
gently combine. Season with salt and freshly ground black pepper, then
cover with a lid, transfer to the oven and cook for 30 mins.

4 Remove from the oven and lay the lamb steaks on top of the veg. Sprinkle
over the crumbled feta and oregano. Return to the oven, uncovered, and
cook for 10 mins until warmed through.

Per serving: 661 cals, 36g fat, 15g sat fat, 9g total sugars, 1.9g salt

Serves 4
Prep time: 15 mins
Cook time: 1 hour
5 mins

Ready in 1 hour 20 mins

All-in-one baked sausages with lentils

Transform sausages into a hearty family supper with the addition of lots of fresh vegetables and a tin of lentils

454g pack Butcher's Choice reduced fat pork sausages by Sainsbury's
1 tbsp olive oil
2 celery sticks, trimmed and cut into 2.5cm pieces
4 carrots, peeled and halved lengthways and cut into small chunks
1 red onion, cut into wedges
1 red pepper, deseeded and sliced

2 cloves garlic, sliced
500ml beef stock, hot
1 tsp Dijon mustard
410g tin green lentils by Sainsbury's, drained and rinsed
¼ x 15g pack fresh thyme by Sainsbury's, leaves picked
2 fresh or dried bay leaves

1 Preheat the oven to 200ºC, fan 180ºC, gas 6. Put the sausages in an ovenproof baking dish. Add the oil and turn the sausages to coat. Bake for 10 mins before adding all the vegetables and garlic. Season with salt and freshly ground black pepper and stir together until combined. Return to the oven to cook for 30 mins.

2 Mix the hot stock with the mustard and pour over the sausages and vegetables. Add the lentils and herbs, then stir everything together. Cover carefully with foil and cook for a further 20-25 mins, taking the foil off for the final 10 mins. Remove the bay leaves before serving.

Per serving: 534 cals, 22.9g fat, 8.9g sat fat, 14.1g total sugars, 2.1g salt

A different way
with sausages the
family will love

Serves 4
Prep time: 10-15 mins
Cook time: 1 hour
20 mins

1 of 5
A-DAY

Ready in 1 hour 35 mins

Shepherd's pie

A classic crowd-pleasing dish with meat, veg and potato all in one!

2 tbsp olive oil

500g lamb mince

1 onion, very finely chopped

4 cloves garlic, crushed

1 tsp dried oregano

2 carrots, peeled and finely chopped

2 celery sticks, trimmed and finely chopped

2 tbsp plain flour

1 tbsp tomato purée

400ml lamb stock, hot

2 tbsp Worcestershire sauce

400g pack ready mashed potato by Sainsbury's

25g mature Cheddar, finely grated

1 Heat 1 tbsp oil in a shallow flameproof casserole (about 1.5 litres), over a high heat. Add the mince and fry for 5 mins until it begins to brown. Remove from the pan and set aside.

2 Add the remaining 1 tbsp olive oil to the casserole. Reduce the heat to medium and add the onion. Fry for 1 min, then add the garlic, oregano, carrots and celery. Fry for 5 mins until the vegetables begin to soften and turn translucent.

3 Return the mince to the casserole and stir through the flour and tomato purée until they are evenly distributed. Cook for 2-3 mins, then pour over the stock and Worcestershire sauce. Reduce the heat to low, cover and simmer for 30 mins, stirring occasionally to prevent it sticking to the bottom of the casserole. Season with salt and freshly ground black pepper.

4 Meanwhile, preheat the oven to 190°C, fan 170°C, gas 5. Gently dollop the mashed potato over the filling, using a fork to give the mash a little texture. Sprinkle over the cheese and bake for 30 mins, or until the potato begins to brown. Serve immediately.

Per serving: 582 cals, 34g fat, 16g sat fat, 10g total sugars, 1.3g salt

Who can resist this traditional British favourite?

Ready in 1 hour 40 mins

Lamb kleftiko

Serves 4
Prep time: 10 mins
Cook time: 1 hour 30 mins

2 of 5 A-DAY

This lightly spiced, slow-cooked lamb dish is a favourite in Greece

500g potatoes, cut into wedges
2 x 300g packs diced lamb by Sainsbury's
2 onions, sliced
3 cloves garlic, roughly chopped
2 tsp cumin seeds
1 tsp dried oregano

1 tsp ground cinnamon
28g pack fresh flat-leaf parsley by Sainsbury's, leaves picked and chopped
200ml lamb stock, hot
4 large tomatoes, thickly sliced

1 Preheat the oven to 200°C, fan 180°C, gas 6. Cut a piece of kitchen foil to twice the length of a 2-litre baking dish. Lay the foil inside the dish and lay a piece of baking parchment on top of the foil. Place the potatoes in the dish with the lamb, onions, garlic cloves, cumin, oregano, cinnamon, half the parsley and all of the stock. Mix well.

2 Layer the tomatoes over the top. Season with salt and freshly ground black pepper, then fold over the foil and baking parchment and secure by crimping the edges. Bake for 1½ hours, or until the lamb is tender and the vegetables are cooked.

3 Cut off and remove the top of the foil and baking parchment and sprinkle over the remaining parsley to serve.

Per serving: 583 cals, 30g fat, 14g sat fat, 8.8g total sugars, 0.6g salt

Lamb fried rice

Cook 2 x 250g packs Sainsbury's microwaveable long grain rice following pack instructions. Heat a large frying pan and dry fry 90g cashew nuts until golden, then remove and set aside. Add 1 tbsp oil to the hot pan, then add ½ tsp ground cumin and 300g leftover roast lamb, torn into strips. Lightly fry, then stir in the rice and a 410g tin drained chickpeas and cook for 2 mins. Stir in 125g chopped dried apricots, the cashew nuts and ½ x 31g pack fresh coriander, chopped. Heat through and serve.

Serves 4 Ready: 20 mins Prep time: 5 mins Cook time: 15 mins

Per serving: 605 cals, 23g fat, 5.3g sat fat, 13g total sugars, 0.12g salt

A perfect parcel of tender lamb and tasty veg

Serves 4
Prep time: 10 mins
Cook time: 1 hour
30 mins

Ready in 1 hour 40 mins

Pork, potato & apple bake

This easy dish is great for entertaining - just bring the roasting tin to the table and let everyone serve themselves

1 onion, sliced

3 Braeburn apples, peeled, cored and thickly sliced

1 kg Maris Piper potatoes, peeled and sliced

500ml chicken stock, hot

4 tsp fennel seeds, crushed

1 tbsp olive oil

4 pork loin steaks

270g pack Taste the Difference Vittoria vine tomatoes

1 Preheat the oven to 220ºC, fan 200ºC, gas 7. Put the onion, apples and potatoes into a roasting tin. Season with salt and freshly ground black pepper and mix to combine, making sure it's evenly spread out.

2 Pour over the stock, cover with foil and bake for 30 mins. Remove the foil and reduce the oven temperature to 200ºC, fan 180ºC, gas 6, then cook for a further 45 mins until the potatoes are tender.

3 Meanwhile, mix the crushed fennel seeds with the olive oil and rub over the pork loin steaks.

4 Add the steaks to the roasting tin along with the tomatoes, and cook for 15 mins until the pork is cooked through.

Per serving: 517 cals, 12g fat, 3.7g sat fat, 20g total sugars, 1.4g salt

Serves 4
Prep time: 10-15 mins
Cook time: 1 hour
30 mins

Ready in 1 hour 45 mins

Chilli con carne

A great family favourite, serve this with ready-baked jacket potatoes or microwaveable rice to make it easy - or add tortilla chips for a bit of crunch

2 tbsp olive oil
500g pack lean British beef steak mince by Sainsbury's
2 red onions, roughly chopped
4 cloves garlic, sliced
1 tsp ground cumin
2 tsp chilli powder
1 tsp paprika
2 red peppers, deseeded and roughly diced

410g tin red kidney beans by Sainsbury's, drained and rinsed
390g carton chopped Italian tomatoes in tomato juice by Sainsbury's
175ml red wine
300ml vegetable stock, hot
4 tbsp chopped fresh coriander
4 ready-baked jacket potatoes, to serve
4 tbsp soured cream

1 Heat 1 tbsp olive oil over a high heat in a large, flameproof casserole. Add the mince and cook for 5-10 mins until browned and any liquid has evaporated. Remove from the pan and set aside.

2 Put the remaining olive oil in the casserole and return it to a medium heat. Add the red onions and cook for 2-3 mins until beginning to turn golden. Add the garlic, cumin, chilli powder, paprika and red peppers to the casserole and fry for a further 2-3 mins.

3 Return the browned mince to the pan with the drained kidney beans, chopped tomatoes, red wine and vegetable stock. Season with salt and freshly ground black pepper.

4 Bring to the boil, then reduce the heat and simmer, uncovered, for 1 hour, stirring regularly. Stir through half the coriander, then serve with the jacket potatoes, cooked according to pack instructions, and garnished with the soured cream and the remaining coriander.

Per serving: 597 cals, 25g fat, 11g sat fat, 15g total sugars, 1.1g salt

Cook's tip
You could also serve this with rice – use 2 x 250g packs of Sainsbury's microwaveable long grain rice to make enough for 4 people.

Ready in 2 hours

Beef massaman

A fantastic, Thai-style all-in-one curry made with beef and potatoes

Serves 6
Prep time: 15 mins
Cook time: 1 hour
45 mins

2 tbsp olive oil
2 x 457g packs lean casserole steak
by Sainsbury's, cut into 2-3cm chunks
1 onion, finely sliced
1 red pepper, deseeded and sliced
3 tbsp massaman curry paste by Sainsbury's
500g baby potatoes, peeled and halved

1 cinnamon stick
3 star anise
400ml coconut milk
2 tbsp fish sauce
2 tsp light brown sugar
100g peanuts, roughly chopped
3 spring onions, trimmed and sliced

1   Heat 1 tbsp olive oil in a large, heavy based pot, over a high heat. Add the diced steak and fry until it begins to colour – you may need to do this in batches. Transfer the meat to a plate and set aside.

2   Add the remaining olive oil to the pot and fry the onion and pepper for 5 mins, until golden. Stir through the curry paste, potatoes, cinnamon stick and star anise. Cook for 2-3 mins, then stir in the coconut milk, 250ml water, the fish sauce, sugar and peanuts. Return the beef to the pan.

3   Reduce the heat to low and simmer the curry, covered, for 1 1/4 hours, until the meat is tender. Remove the lid and boil over a high heat for 10 mins, to thicken the sauce. Serve, garnished with the spring onions.

Per serving: 581 cals, 26g fat, 12g sat fat, 9.1g total sugars, 1.6g salt

Beef with black bean & broccoli

Heat a wok over a high heat and spray with a little oil. Stir fry 400g thinly sliced rump steak for 2 mins, then set aside. Add more oil to the wok, then stir fry 10 sliced spring onions and 2 x 120g packs halved shiitake mushrooms for 4 mins. Add 2 x 200g packs Tenderstem broccoli, halved, and 100ml water. Cover and cook until the broccoli is tender. Stir in a 175g pack black bean stir fry sauce by Sainsbury's, then add the beef back into the wok, warm through and serve with cooked microwaveable rice.

Serves 4   Ready: 20 mins   Prep time: 10 mins   Cook time: 10 mins

Per serving: 519 cals, 18g fat, 6.7g sat fat, 7.4g total sugars, 0.91g salt

Serves 4
Prep time: 15 mins
Cook time: 2 hours
15 mins, plus resting

Ready in 2 hours 30 mins

Lamb with squash & pearl barley

A hearty lamb stew loaded with lovely sweet flavours

1.5kg boned rolled shoulder of lamb by Sainsbury's
20g pack fresh rosemary by Sainsbury's, leaves picked and finely chopped
28g pack fresh mint by Sainsbury's, roughly chopped
Zest and juice of 1 lemon
2 tbsp olive oil

1 tbsp clear honey
1 onion, thickly sliced
1 butternut squash, peeled, deseeded and cut into 2cm cubes
350ml chicken or lamb stock, hot
250ml white wine
200g pearl barley by Sainsbury's
50g feta, crumbled

1 Preheat the oven to 200ºC, fan 180ºC, gas 6. With a sharp knife, score the skin of the meat. In a bowl, combine the rosemary, half the mint, the lemon zest and juice, half the olive oil and the honey. Season with salt and freshly ground black pepper, then rub half of the mixture over the lamb.

2 Heat the remaining oil in a large, deep flameproof casserole over a medium heat, cook the onion for 5 mins, then add the squash and remaining herb mixture and cook, stirring occasionally, for a further 5 mins. Remove from the heat.

3 Pour the stock and wine into the casserole, and place the lamb on top of the vegetables. Cover and cook in the oven for 2 hours.

4 Halfway through the cooking time, remove from the oven, pour the pearl barley into the liquid around the meat and add 200ml boiling water. Use a spoon to make sure the pearl barley is evenly distributed, then return to the oven, uncovered, for the final hour. Check after 30 mins, and cover if the meat is browning too much.

5 Remove the meat from the casserole and rest for 10 mins before carving. Stir the feta and the remaining mint through the squash and pearl barley, then serve with the sliced lamb.

Per serving: 695 cals, 39g fat, 17g sat fat, 16g total sugars, 1.6g salt

Serves 6
Prep time: 15 mins
Cook time: 2 hrs
20 mins

Ready in 2 hours 35 mins

Beef bourguignon

A slow-cooked dish of beef and vegetables simmered in red wine, this French recipe has plenty of deep, rich flavours to savour

3 tbsp olive oil

700g beef braising steak, roughly cut up

300g pack diced onions by Sainsbury's

4 cubes frozen crushed garlic by Sainsbury's

103g pack Italian cubetti di pancetta for cooking by Sainsbury's

250g pack closed-cup chestnut mushrooms, by Sainsbury's, quartered

3 tbsp plain flour

500g baby potatoes, large ones halved

3 parsnips, scrubbed and halved lengthways, then cut into chunks

2 carrots, peeled and roughly chopped

3-4 sprigs fresh thyme, plus a few extra thyme leaves to garnish

400ml red wine

400ml beef stock, hot

1   Heat 2 tbsp of the oil in a deep flameproof casserole over a high heat. Sear the beef in batches, until each piece has begun to brown, then set aside.

2   Add the remaining oil to the casserole, along with the onions, garlic and pancetta and fry for 5 mins. Add the mushrooms and continue to fry for a few more mins. Return the beef to the casserole, sprinkle with flour, season with salt and freshly ground black pepper and stir to combine.

3   Add the potatoes, parsnips, carrots, thyme, wine and beef stock to the pot. Bring to a simmer, then reduce the heat, cover and simmer for 2 hours. Every so often, give the stew a good stir to stop it sticking to the bottom of the casserole. If you think it's looking a little dry, add some water.

4   Serve, garnished with a few fresh thyme leaves.

Per serving: 618 cals, 32g fat, 12g sat fat, 11g total sugars, 1.8g salt

Ready in 2 hours 40 mins

Beef, ale & mushroom pie

A British pub classic, this is the perfect winter warmer family treat

Serves 4
Prep time: 10 mins
Cook time: 2 hours 30 mins

600g British beef braising steak, cut into 2-3cm chunks

2 tbsp plain flour

2 tbsp olive oil

2 onions, halved and sliced

2 carrots, scrubbed and cut into 2-3cm crescents

2 celery sticks, trimmed and cut into 2-3cm crescents

250g pack closed-cup chestnut mushrooms by Sainsbury's, sliced thickly

3 cloves garlic, roughly chopped

300ml brown ale

400ml beef stock, hot

3 sprigs fresh thyme, leaves picked

1 tsp English mustard

375g pack ready-rolled light puff pastry by Sainsbury's

1 medium egg, lightly beaten

1 Preheat the oven to 180°C, fan 160°C, gas 4. In a bowl, mix together the braising steak and 1 tbsp of the flour. Heat 1 tbsp of the oil in a 1.5-litre shallow flameproof casserole (about 23cm in diameter), add the beef and cook for 2-3 mins, until browned. You may need to do this in batches. Remove the beef from the pan and set aside.

2 Heat the remaining oil in the pan and cook the onions, carrots and celery for 10 mins. Stir in the beef, remaining flour, mushrooms, garlic, ale, beef stock, thyme and mustard. Stir well, season with salt and freshly ground black pepper, then bring to the boil, cover with a tight-fitting lid and cook in the oven for 1 3/4 hours, stirring occasionally. If the liquid is looking a little low, add a splash of water.

3 Meanwhile, cut the pastry into a circle the same size as your casserole pan and put it into the fridge to chill.

4 Remove the casserole from the oven and increase the temperature to 200°C, fan 180°C, gas 6. Place the puff pastry circle on top of the pie filling. Brush with the beaten egg, then cook in the oven for 15-20 mins until the top is golden and the stew is bubbling underneath.

Per serving: 751 cals, 41g fat, 17g sat fat, 12g total sugars, 1.8g salt

Serves 4
Prep time: 15 mins
Cook time: 2 hours
30 mins

Ready in 2 hours 45 mins

Steak fusion stew

This long, slow stew has an Asian twist with an infusion of fresh chillies, ginger, star anise and soy sauce. Serve it with rice to soak up the wonderful juices

1 tbsp olive oil	50ml light soy sauce
600g braising steak, cut into large pieces	250ml red wine
3 onions, roughly chopped	500ml beef stock, hot
500g carrots, peeled and roughly chopped	2 x 250g packs microwaveable long
30g ginger, peeled and finely sliced	grain rice by Sainsbury's, cooked to
3 cloves garlic, finely sliced	pack instructions
4 star anise	½ x 31g pack fresh coriander
1½ red chillies, deseeded and cut into strips	by Sainsbury's

1 Heat the oil in a frying pan, then brown the steak pieces and set aside.

2 In the same pan, fry the onions and carrots over a gentle heat for 10 mins, until slightly tender. Stir in the ginger, garlic, star anise and 1 chilli, and cook for 1 min, then pour in the liquids and add the beef back into the pan. Make sure the liquid covers the meat – if it doesn't, top up with hot water.

3 Cook gently for 1½ hours, then increase the heat and cook for a further 30 mins, until the liquid is thick and reduced by a third. Serve with the rice, garnished with coriander and the remaining chilli.

Per serving: 730 cals, 30g fat, 13g sat fat, 19g total sugars, 2.9g salt

Beef stroganoff

Heat 1 tbsp oil in a large pan and add 1 sliced onion. Cook over a low heat for 5 mins, then add 500g mushrooms (we used shiitake, chestnut and oyster), and increase the heat to medium. Cook for 5 more mins, adding 1 chopped clove garlic for the final 1 min. Stir in 300g leftover roast beef, cubed, 200ml crème fraîche and 100ml chicken stock. Reduce to a simmer for 2 mins. Cook 2 x 250g packs microwaveable basmati rice to pack instructions. Serve with the stroganoff and chopped parsley to garnish.

Serves 4 Ready: 25 mins Prep time: 10 mins Cook time: 15 mins

Per serving: 560 cals, 24.4g fat, 15.7g sat fat, 4.9g total sugars, 0.67g salt

'The meat will just fall
apart when you cut into it

Serves 6
with leftover roast pork
Prep time: 15 mins
Cook time: 2 hours
20 mins, plus resting

Ready in 2 hours 45 mins

Stuffed roast pork with baked couscous

Let the oven take the strain with this easy-prep roast pork dish

130g pack apple & herb stuffing mix
by Sainsbury's
4 cloves garlic, crushed
1 large green apple, grated
50g dried apricots, roughly chopped
2kg (approximately) British pork boneless
leg joint by Sainsbury's
½ tsp salt
2 tsp fennel seeds, lightly crushed

4 parsnips, scrubbed and quartered
400g echalion shallots, peeled and
halved lengthways
4 medium carrots, scrubbed, trimmed
and halved lengthways
150g couscous
250ml vegetable stock, hot
2 tbsp roughly chopped fresh
flat-leaf parsley

1 Preheat the oven to 220°C, fan 200°C, gas 7. Make up the stuffing
according to pack instructions in a medium bowl, stirring through the
garlic, apple and apricots. Lay the pork on a board. To create space for
the stuffing, cut down the middle of the joint (towards the skin), then cut
across the flesh halfway on one side, so you have a pocket in the meat.

2 Spread half of the stuffing into the pocket, season with salt and freshly
ground black pepper, then roll up the pork and tie with string (in 4 places)
so the stuffing is in the centre. Roll the other half of the stuffing into small
balls and set aside.

3 Put the joint in a large roasting tin and rub the salt over the skin. Roast for
30 mins. Remove and reduce the heat to 200°C, fan 180°C, gas 6.

4 Nestle the fennel seeds, parsnips, shallots and carrots around the pork,
coating with any fat and return to the oven for a further 1 hour.

5 Remove from the oven and sprinkle the couscous around the pork, using
a large spoon to mix with the roasted vegetables. Pour over the stock; try
not to get any on the crackling. Return the tin to the oven and roast for
a further 50 mins, adding the stuffing balls for the last 20 mins. Rest the
pork for 10 mins, then serve sprinkled with fresh parsley.

Per serving: 631 cals, 23g fat, 8.1g sat fat, 22g total sugars, 1.7g salt

Ready in 2 hours 55 mins

Beef stew with herb dumplings

Slow-cooking makes the beef meltingly tender and the little herby dumplings are the perfect accompaniment

Serves 4
Prep time: 15 mins
Cook time: 2 hours 40 mins

1 tbsp olive oil
1 onion, chopped
457g pack lean diced casserole steak by Sainsbury's
3 carrots, peeled and roughly chopped
1 parsnip, peeled and roughly chopped
1 swede, peeled and roughly chopped

1 ½ tsp dried mixed herbs
390g carton Italian chopped tomatoes in tomato juice by Sainsbury's
1 beef or vegetable stock cube, crumbled
200g self-raising flour
100g unsalted butter, chilled
Fresh flat-leaf parsley, chopped, to garnish

1 Heat the oil in a deep saucepan over a medium heat, then add the onion and fry for a few mins until soft.

2 Add the beef and the rest of the veg. Season with salt and freshly ground black pepper, add 1 tsp mixed herbs, then fry for 10 mins. Stir in the tomatoes, 1 litre water and the crumbled stock cube. Bring to the boil, then turn the heat down and simmer, uncovered, for 2 hours.

3 Meanwhile, place the self-raising flour in a bowl and season with salt and freshly ground black pepper. Grate in the butter and the remaining mixed herbs, then rub together with your finger tips until the mixture looks like breadcrumbs. Gradually mix in small amounts of cold water until it forms a soft dough, then roll into about 12 evenly sized balls.

4 After 2 hours, the stew should be nice and saucy but if it looks a little dry, stir in another 400ml water. Bring to the boil again. Add the dumplings, pushing them beneath the liquid. Cover and simmer for 20 mins until the dumplings are puffed up and cooked through, then serve with the freshly chopped parsley sprinkled over.

Per serving: 694 cals, 28g fat, 14g sat fat, 19g total sugars, 1.9g salt

Serves 4
Prep time: 15 mins
Cook time: 4 hours 15 mins

Ready in 4 hours 30 mins

Indian lamb shanks

After long, slow cooking at a low temperature, the lamb will simply melt off the bone. A dollop of yogurt adds a sharp richness to the spinach and potatoes

4 lamb shanks
1 garlic bulb, cloves separated, peeled and halved lengthways
20g pack rosemary by Sainsbury's, leaves picked
3 tbsp Goan masala curry paste by Sainsbury's
1 tsp garam masala

1 tsp ground cumin
700ml lamb stock
2 onions, cut into wedges
1kg pack baby potatoes by Sainsbury's
335g pack cherry tomatoes by Sainsbury's
260g pack young leaf spinach by Sainsbury's
250g Greek-style natural yogurt

1 Preheat the oven to 150°C, fan 130° C, gas 2. Using a sharp knife, make small insertions evenly around the lamb shanks. Stud the lamb shanks with half of the garlic cloves and half of the rosemary leaves, then place into a large deep roasting tray.

2 In a large bowl, mix together the Goan curry paste, garam masala, cumin and lamb stock. Then add the onions, the remaining garlic cloves and the remaining rosemary.

3 Pour into the oven tray with the lamb shanks and cook for 3 hours. Then add the potatoes, tomatoes, 200ml water and cook for a further 1¼ hours. The lamb should be really tender and the potatoes should be cooked through.

4 Stir in the spinach and yogurt and return to the oven for 3 mins to wilt.

Per serving: 725 cals, 30g fat, 12g sat fat, 16g total sugars, 1.6g salt

fish
& seafood

Ready in 15 mins

Oriental steamed fish

Serves 4
Prep time: 5 mins
Cook time: 10 mins

Steaming fish keeps in all its goodness and succulence. The chilli, ginger and lemon in this recipe work brilliantly with the delicate flavour of the cod

4 pak choi, leaves separated
4 cod fillets, each cut in half
1 lemon, sliced into thin rounds
1 red chilli, deseeded and finely sliced
2cm piece root ginger, peeled and cut into matchsticks

2 x 250g packs microwaveable basmati rice by Sainsbury's
¼ x 31g pack fresh coriander by Sainsbury's, roughly chopped
2 tbsp sesame oil
2 tbsp light soy sauce

1 Put the pak choi leaves in the base of a large steamer and lay the fish on top. Top with the lemon slices, chilli and ginger. Cover with a tight-fitting lid and sit over a pan of simmering water. Steam for 10 mins until the fish is cooked through.

2 Meanwhile, cook the rice according to pack instructions, then stir through the chopped coriander.

3 Mix the sesame oil and soy sauce together and drizzle over the fish. Serve the fish and pak choi with the coriander rice.

Per serving: 352 cals, 7.9g fat, 1.1g sat fat, 3.0g total sugars, 1.3g salt

Smoked salmon carbonara

In a large pan, cook 250g spaghetti in boiling water for 9-10 mins, adding in 200g fine beans and 300g frozen peas for the last 4 mins. Drain, reserving 150ml pasta water. In a bowl, whisk together 3 medium eggs, 50g grated parmesan, 2 tbsp double cream, 1 chopped clove garlic, 120g smoked salmon, torn, and 2 tbsp chopped chives. Pour into the pasta with the reserved water and stir over a low heat for 1-2 mins, until the sauce thickens. Serve with extra parmesan and chopped chives to garnish.

Serves 4 Ready: 20 mins Prep time: 5 mins Cook time: 15 mins

Per serving: 505 cals, 18g fat, 7.3g sat fat, 5.6g total sugars, 1.8g salt

A very quick,
and tasty, fish dish

Ready in 20 mins

Chinese prawn stir fry

Serves 4
Prep time: 10 mins
Cook time: 10 mins

A classic that couldn't be easier – just chop and toss! You could even leave out the soy, honey and sesame oil and replace with your favourite stir fry sauces

410g pack free range fresh egg noodles by Sainsbury's (ready cooked)

2 tbsp olive oil

1 red chilli, deseeded and finely chopped

2 cloves garlic, finely sliced

3cm piece root ginger, peeled and grated

225g pack Taste the Difference raw peeled jumbo king prawns

200g pack Sainsbury's Tenderstem broccoli, halved lengthways

1 red pepper, deseeded and sliced

200g pack sugar snap peas by Sainsbury's

1 carrot, peeled and sliced into ribbons

5 spring onions, trimmed and sliced

2 tbsp light soy sauce

1 tbsp honey

1 tbsp sesame oil

1 Pierce the pack of noodles with a knife, microwave on high for 1-2 mins, then set aside.

2 Meanwhile, heat 1 tbsp of the olive oil in a wok (or frying pan) over a high heat and cook the chilli, garlic, ginger and prawns. Stir frequently for 2-3 mins until the prawns are pink and cooked through. Transfer to a bowl and keep warm.

3 Add the remaining 1 tbsp olive oil to the wok and then toss in the broccoli, red pepper, sugar snaps, carrot and spring onions. Stir fry for 3 mins, until slightly tender.

4 Mix the soy sauce, honey and sesame oil together and drizzle into the wok. Stir well to coat the veg, then add the prawn mixture along with the noodles to the pan. Toss everything together and cook for 2 mins, until it's all heated through. Serve immediately.

Per serving: 368 cals, 12g fat, 1.8g sat fat, 13g total sugars, 1.9g salt

Juicy prawns and veg in a tasty sweet sauce – irresistible!

Serves 4
Prep time: 10 mins
Cook time: 10 mins

Ready in 20 mins

Mussels with parsley & wine

These juicy little morsels are at their best in the colder months – and they're ready in just 20 minutes. Serve with plenty of crusty French bread

2 x 1kg bags fresh mussels, in their shells
1 tbsp olive oil
1 onion, finely chopped
2 fresh bay leaves
8 sprigs fresh thyme
2 cloves garlic, chopped

300ml Sainsbury's house medium white wine
100ml single cream
28g pack fresh flat-leaf parsley by Sainsbury's, leaves picked and chopped
French bread, to serve

1 Scrub the mussels well in a large bowl of cold water, removing the beards and any barnacles. Discard any with broken shells or any that don't close tight when tapped on a hard surface.

2 Heat the oil in a large saucepan over a medium heat. Add the onion, bay leaves and thyme, and cook for 4 mins. Stir in the garlic and cook for a further 1 min.

3 Pour over the wine and simmer for 1 min. Tip in the mussels, then cover the pan and allow them to steam, shaking the pan every now and then, for about 3-4 mins, or until all the mussels have opened. Discard any that remain shut.

4 Stir in the cream and parsley and serve in warm bowls with the bread.

Per serving: 528 cals, 12.9g fat, 4.3g sat fat, 6.8g total sugars, 3.04g salt

Cook's tip
This dish also makes a great starter – the quantities in this recipe will serve 8 as a starter, or simply halve the ingredients to serve 4.

Ready in 25 mins

Singapore noodles

The popular Asian egg noodle dish made with prawns

Serves 4
Prep time: 10 mins
Cook time: 10-15 mins

1 tbsp vegetable oil

1 onion, finely sliced

2 cubes frozen crushed garlic by Sainsbury's

1 red chilli, deseeded and finely chopped

2 tsp mild curry powder

3 tbsp light soy sauce

300g pack Oriental vegetable stir fry by Sainsbury's

4 spring onions, trimmed and thinly sliced, plus a few extra to garnish

225g Taste the Difference frozen raw and peeled jumbo king prawns, defrosted

410g pack free range fresh egg noodles by Sainsbury's (ready cooked)

2 medium eggs, beaten

1 lime, cut into wedges

1 Heat the oil over a high heat in a large wok or frying pan. Add the onion, garlic and chilli, and fry for 2-3 mins. Add the curry powder and continue to fry for a further 1 min. Pour over the soy sauce and stir well.

2 Add the vegetable stir fry pack, spring onions and prawns and stir fry for another 2-3 mins until everything is piping hot and the prawns are pink and cooked through.

3 Meanwhile, pierce the pack of noodles with a knife and microwave on high for 1-2 mins.

4 Stir the noodles into the vegetable mix, then push all the ingredients to one side while you pour the beaten eggs into the other side of the pan. Cook, as you would scrambled eggs, then combine the eggs with all the other ingredients in the pan.

5 Serve immediately, garnished with the extra spring onions and a squeeze of lime juice.

Per serving: 362 cals, 14g fat, 2.1g sat fat, 7g total sugars, 2.4g salt

Ready in 30 mins

Asian fish & rice stew

Serves 4
Prep time: 10 mins
Cook time: 20 mins

This recipe is loaded with fresh flavours and a good bit of heat!

1 tbsp olive oil

1 onion, chopped

500g sweet potato, peeled and cut into cubes

½ x 10g pack korma curry kit by Sainsbury's

1 red chilli, deseeded and finely sliced

200ml reduced-fat coconut milk

1.4 litres vegetable stock, hot

300g basmati rice

1 red pepper, deseeded and sliced

320g pack fish pie mix by Sainsbury's

200g frozen peas

Zest and juice of 1 lime

1 Heat the oil in a large pan and cook the onion and sweet potato for 5 mins. Add the korma spices and half of the chilli, and cook for a further 1 min.

2 Add the coconut milk, stock and rice, and bring to the boil. Reduce to a simmer and cook, covered, for 8 mins. Stir in the red pepper, fish pie mix and peas. Put the lid back on and cook for a further 5 mins or until the fish is cooked through.

3 Season with salt and freshly ground black pepper, then stir through the lime zest and juice, and scatter the remaining chilli over the top.

Per serving: 636 cals, 15g fat, 6.4g sat fat, 14g total sugars, 1.8g salt

Sweet & sour prawns

Stir fry 1 diced onion and 1 sliced red pepper in 1 tbsp oil in a wok for 3 mins. Add 1 crushed clove of garlic, a knob of ginger, chopped, 1 chopped red chilli and 4 sliced spring onions for the last 1 min. Add 100g sugar snap peas, 180g raw king prawns, a 227g tin pineapple slices with juice and a 175ml pack sweet & sour stir fry sauce. Cook for 4 mins, then serve with 2 x 250g packs microwaveable long grain rice, cooked to pack instructions. Garnish with 1 chopped spring onion and lime wedges.

Serves 4 Ready: 20 mins Prep time: 10 mins Cook time: 10 mins

Per serving: 374 cals, 4.9g fat, 0.7g sat fat, 27g total sugars, 0.82g salt

Serves 4
Prep time: 5-10 mins
Cook time: 25 mins

2 of 5 A-DAY

Ready in 35 mins

Spiced seafood paella

Irresistibly smoky with a generous mix of fish and shellfish, this is an easy-cook paella that's packed with flavour

1 tbsp olive oil
1 onion, finely chopped
2 tsp smoked paprika
1 tsp cayenne pepper
1 tsp turmeric
½ x 500g pack basmati rice by Sainsbury's
200ml white wine
390g pack Italian chopped tomatoes with basil, chilli & oregano by Sainsbury's
500ml fish stock, hot

500g pack Just Cook Scottish mussels with a garlic sauce by Sainsbury's
260g pack skinless and boneless cod fillet by Sainsbury's
225g pack Taste the Difference frozen raw peeled jumbo king prawns, defrosted
300g petits pois peas
100g bag baby leaf spinach by Sainsbury's
Lemon wedges, to serve

1 In a large flameproof casserole, heat the oil over a medium heat. Cook the onion for 5 mins, then stir in the paprika, cayenne pepper, turmeric and rice. Cook for 3 mins, then add the wine.

2 Allow the wine to cook for 2 mins, then add the chopped tomatoes and stock. Bring to the boil, then reduce the heat, cover and simmer for 5 mins. Season with salt and freshly ground black pepper.

3 Add the mussels (discard any that are cracked or don't close when tapped on a hard surface) and cook, covered for 3 mins. Add the cod, prawns and peas to the pan, cover and cook for a further 5 mins. Discard any mussels that don't open after cooking. Finally, stir through the spinach and allow it to wilt before serving with lemon wedges to squeeze over.

Per serving: 515 cals, 11g fat, 3.7g sat fat, 9.1g total sugars, 3.5g salt

Cook's tip
If you can't find the frozen prawns, fresh, raw or cooked peeled prawns will be fine.

Serves 4
Prep time: 10 mis
Cook time: 30 mins

1 OF 5
A-DAY

Ready in 40 mins

Fish pie

Our take on the classic fish pie uses some of Sainsbury's fantastic ready-to-go ingredients to cut your prep time down to a minimum

2 tbsp olive oil
15g unsalted butter
10 spring onions, trimmed and sliced
3 cloves garlic, crushed
600ml semi-skimmed milk
40g plain flour
2 tsp Dijon mustard
300g broccoli, cut into very small florets

200g frozen garden peas
2 x 320g packs fish pie mix by Sainsbury's
½ x 28g pack fresh flat-leaf parsley by Sainsbury's, chopped
400g pack ready mashed potato by Sainsbury's
25g mature British Cheddar, finely grated

1 Preheat the grill to medium. Heat the oil and butter in a large shallow flameproof casserole (about 1.5 litre) and cook the spring onions and garlic for 3-4 mins. Mix 3 tbsp of the milk into the flour, then stir into the casserole with the remaining milk and bring to a gentle simmer, whisking all the time. Bring to the boil and cook for 2 mins until the sauce has thickened.

2 Add in the Dijon mustard, broccoli florets, garden peas, and fish pie mix and cook for 5-6 mins. Then stir in the parsley and season with salt and freshly ground black pepper.

3 Meanwhile, cook the mashed potato in the microwave for 2-3 mins according to pack instructions, then gently spread over the fish pie mixture. Sprinkle over the cheese and place under the grill for 5-10 mins, until golden.

Per serving: 547 cals, 25g fat, 8.3g sat fat, 11g total sugars, 2g salt

Cook's tip
You can make this recipe go further and serve 6 by adding 4 quartered hard-boiled eggs and a 180g pack of prawns.

Serves 4
Prep time: 5 mins
Cook time: 40 mins

1 of 5 A-DAY

Ready in 45 mins

Smoked mackerel risotto

The rich flavour of hot-smoked mackerel fillets adds plenty of punch to this unusual risotto that uses just a few simple ingredients

1 tbsp olive oil
1 onion, finely chopped
250g risotto rice
1.5 litres chicken stock, hot
250g pack hot-smoked mackerel fillets by Sainsbury's, torn into small pieces

6 spring onions, trimmed and finely chopped
260g pack young spinach by Sainsbury's

1 Heat the oil in a large pan. Add the onion and cook for 5-10 mins until soft, then add the risotto rice and cook for another 1 min.

2 Begin adding the stock, a ladleful at a time, stirring until the stock is absorbed before adding the next ladleful. Continue until all the stock is used and the rice is cooked through (about 20-25 mins).

3 Add the mackerel, spring onions and spinach to the risotto. Stir until the spinach has wilted, then serve.

Per serving: 549 cals, 24.7g fat, 9.7g sat fat, 3.9g total sugars, 0.5g salt

Prawn & spinach omelette

Separate 4 medium eggs and whisk the whites and yolks in different bowls. Preheat the grill to medium. Cook 2 chopped cloves garlic with 1 chopped red chilli in 1 tbsp olive oil in a 22cm ovenproof frying pan. Stir in 200g young spinach and cook for 2-3 mins, until the liquid has evaporated. Season. Pour into the egg yolk bowl with 180g cooked king prawns, and 4 tbsp double cream, then fold in the egg whites. Pour into the pan. Cook for 3 mins, then grill for 3-4 mins. Once set, serve with chopped chives and grated parmesan.

Serves 4 Ready: 20 mins Prep time: 5 mins Cook time: 15 mins

Per serving: 233 cals, 17g fat, 7.3g sat fat, 0.7g total sugars, 0.96g salt

An easy risotto to make with a delicious fishy twist ,

Serves 4
Prep time: 10 mins
Cook time: 40-45 mins

Ready in 55 mins

Mediterranean fish traybake

For a fish supper with a twist, try this saucy salmon dish that combines summery flavours including basil, olives, lemon and thyme

1 kg baby potatoes, large ones cut in half
500g courgettes, trimmed and chopped
1 red onion, cut into wedges
1 tbsp olive oil
2 x 240g packs responsibly sourced boneless Scottish salmon fillets by Sainsbury's

1 lemon, skin peeled
4 sprigs fresh thyme
4 sprigs fresh flat-leaf parsley
2 x 390g cartons Italian chopped tomatoes in tomato juice
100g pitted black olives
1/2 x 28g pack fresh basil by Sainsbury's

1 Preheat the oven to 200°C, fan 180°C, gas 6.

2 Put the potatoes, courgettes and onion into a large roasting tray. Drizzle with the olive oil, season with salt and freshly ground black pepper and toss to coat. Bake for 30 mins.

3 Meanwhile, make 2-3 slits in the skin of each salmon fillet, then stuff with small pieces of the lemon peel, and the thyme and parsley sprigs.

4 Remove the tray from the oven, pour over the chopped tomatoes and scatter over the olives and half the basil. Top with the salmon fillets, skin-side up. Return to the oven and cook for 10-15 mins until the salmon is cooked through. Remove from the oven and serve garnished with the remaining basil.

Per serving: 530 cals, 21.5g fat, 4.9g sat fat, 11.9g total sugars, 0.67g salt

Ready in 1 hour

Salmon & cherry tomato cannelloni

Here's a different take on the traditional baked cannelloni – it uses salmon and veg instead of a meat sauce and the tubes are standing rather than flat

Serves 6
Prep time: 10-15 mins
Cook time: 45 mins

1 tbsp olive oil
1 onion, finely chopped
1 courgette, trimmed and finely cubed
335g pack cherry tomatoes by Sainsbury's
½ tbsp light brown soft sugar
2 x 500g cartons passata with onion & garlic by Sainsbury's
100ml red wine

2 x 240g packs skinless and boneless salmon fillets by Sainsbury's, chopped into small pieces
250g pack cannelloni tubes by Sainsbury's
350g pot spinach & ricotta sauce by Sainsbury's
125g pack be good to yourself mozzarella, torn

1 Preheat the oven to 180°C, fan 160°C, gas 4. Heat the oil in a deep 2.5 litre flameproof casserole on the hob and cook the onion for 5 mins. Add the courgette, cherry tomatoes and sugar. Cook for a further 5 mins, then add the passata and red wine. Bring to the boil and cook for 5 mins before adding in the salmon pieces.

2 Cook for a further 5 mins on the hob, then arrange the cannelloni tubes vertically down into the pan, making sure the tubes fit tightly, with the sauce in the casserole fitting inside the tubes.

3 Pour over the spinach & ricotta sauce and top with the torn mozzarella. Place in the oven, covered, for 12 mins, then remove the lid and cook for a further 10 mins, until cooked through and golden on top.

Per serving: 495 cals, 17g fat, 6.5g sat fat, 16g total sugars, 1.6g salt

Ready in 1 hour

Sea bass, tomato & new potato bake

Serves 4
Prep time: 10-15 mins
Cook time: 45 mins

This is a fantastic dish for entertaining, full of wonderful colours and flavours. A quick salsa verde gives it a tasty finishing touch

1kg potatoes, peeled and cut into small cubes (about 1-2cm cubed)
2 tbsp olive oil
2 x 180g packs 2 boneless sea bass fillets by Sainsbury's
300g asparagus spears, trimmed
4 mint sprigs

2 lemons, 1 very thinly sliced and the zest and juice of the other
335g pack cherry tomatoes by Sainsbury's
1 tbsp capers, rinsed and roughly chopped
150g pot Italian salsa al pesto by Sainsbury's

1 Preheat the oven to 200°C, fan 180°C, gas 6. Place the potatoes in a baking tray with 1 tbsp oil and bake for 35 mins.

2 Place a sea bass fillet, skin-side up, on a board, then put 3 asparagus spears, 1 mint sprig and a lemon slice on top. Roll up the fillet, with the skin on the inside. Secure with a cocktail stick. Repeat with the other 3 fillets.

3 Once the potatoes have cooked for 35 mins and are beginning to turn golden, arrange the fish fillets and tomatoes on top of the potatoes. Add the remaining lemon slices to the tray, and sprinkle over the lemon zest. Bake for a further 8 mins.

4 Meanwhile, make the salsa verde. In a small bowl, mix together the juice of 1 lemon, the chopped capers and the pesto with 1 tbsp water.

5 Serve the fish and potatoes with the salsa verde drizzled over.

Per serving: 570 cals, 29g fat, 6.2g sat fat, 6.1g total sugars, 1.2g salt

Cook's tip
Sea bass fillets freeze well, so they're great for a standby dinner. They will keep for up to 1 month; just defrost overnight in the fridge.

Ready in 1 hour 5 mins

Baked salmon with watercress sauce

A fantastic recipe to feed a crowd. Ask at the Sainsbury's fish counter for a whole salmon to be filleted to give you two sides with the skin on

Serves 10
Prep time: 15 mins
Cook time: 50 mins

2 sides of salmon, skin on, each weighing about 900g
½ x 28g pack fresh mint by Sainsbury's
½ x 28g pack fresh flat-leaf parsley by Sainsbury's
1 tbsp capers, rinsed
2 x 250g pots roasted vegetable couscous by Sainsbury's

1 lemon, sliced
4 bay leaves
150ml vegetable stock, hot
75g bag watercress by Sainsbury's
300ml half-fat crème fraîche by Sainsbury's
½ tsp French Dijon mustard by Sainsbury's
Juice of ½ lemon

1 Preheat the oven to 200°C, fan 180°C, gas 6. Place a large piece of baking parchment on top of a large piece of kitchen foil, then put one of the salmon sides, skin-side down, on the parchment. Finely chop the mint, parsley and capers together and mix with the couscous. Season with salt and freshly ground black pepper and spoon the couscous onto the fillet.

2 Put the second salmon fillet on top, skin-side up. Lay the lemon slices and bay leaves along the top, then tie the two sides of salmon together in four places with string to secure, making sure the string goes over the lemon and bay leaves to hold in place. Carefully pour over the stock, then fold up the parchment and foil, and scrunch the top to secure into a parcel.

3 Put on a large baking tray and bake for 50 mins or until the salmon is cooked through – push a knife into the salmon to check the fish flakes easily.

4 Meanwhile, snip off most of the stalks from the watercress (reserving a few sprigs for garnish) and whiz the leaves in a food processor with the crème fraîche, mustard, lemon juice and 2 tbsp water until smooth.

5 Carefully lift the salmon onto a board and decorate with the remaining watercress sprigs. If there is any cooking liquor left in the parcel, add it to the watercress sauce. Slice the salmon and serve with the watercress sauce.

Per serving: 457 cals, 25g fat, 8g sat fat, 3.9g total sugars, 1.1g salt

vegetarian

Ready in 25 mins

Gnocchi with blue cheese

Serves 4
Prep time: 5 mins
Cook time: 20 mins

A simple dish that's on the table in a flash – and the combination of broccoli and blue Stilton is a match made in heaven!

1 tbsp olive oil
1 onion, finely sliced
2 cloves garlic, crushed
300g broccoli, cut into florets
150ml crème fraîche

350ml vegetable stock, hot
500g bag fresh gnocchi by Sainsbury's
75g blue Stilton by Sainsbury's, crumbled,
plus a little extra to garnish
200g bag young leaf spinach by Sainsbury's

1 Heat the oil in a large flameproof casserole over a medium heat and add the onion and garlic and cook for 5 mins. Add the broccoli florets and cook for another 5 mins.

2 Stir in the crème fraîche, stock and gnocchi and bring to a gentle simmer. Cook for 5 mins, then add the crumbled Stilton. Stir until the cheese has melted, then add the spinach and let it wilt before serving with the extra blue Stilton crumbled over.

Per serving: 478 cals, 23g fat, 14g sat fat, 5.3g total sugars, 2.7g salt

Spinach, cranberry & cashew pilaf

In a large frying pan, heat 1 tbsp olive oil and cook 1 finely chopped onion, 1 chopped courgette and 2 crushed cloves garlic for 5 mins. Add 250g Sainsbury's long grain & wild rice and 1 tsp medium curry powder, and cook for 1 min, then add 500ml vegetable stock, 1 bay leaf and 75g cranberries. Bring to the boil, cover and cook for 15 mins. Stir in 50g chopped cashew nuts, 1/2 x 31g pack chopped coriander and 200g young leaf spinach. Allow the spinach to wilt for 2 mins. Serve with a sprinkling of coriander.

Serves 4 Ready: 40 mins Prep time: 5-10 mins Cook time: 30 mins

Per serving: 427 cals, 10g fat, 2.2g sat fat, 19g total sugars, 1.1g salt

Ready in 30 mins

Red lentil curry

Served with warm pitta bread, this lightly-spiced lentil curry makes a simple but satisfying family supper

Serves 4
Prep time: 10 mins
Cook time: 20 mins

1 tbsp olive oil
1 onion, finely chopped
31g pack fresh coriander by Sainsbury's, stalks and leaves separated and chopped
2 tbsp Thai red curry paste (suitable for vegetarians)
200g dried red lentils
500ml vegetable stock, hot

390g carton Italian chopped tomatoes with basil and oregano by Sainsbury's
1 cauliflower, broken into small florets
410g tin chickpeas by Sainsbury's, drained and rinsed
210g pack garlic & parsley flatbread by Sainsbury's

1   Preheat the oven to 200°C, fan 180°C, gas 6.

2   Heat the olive oil in a deep ovenproof frying pan. Add the chopped onion, and the coriander stalks and cook for 5 mins, then stir through the Thai red curry paste.

3   Add the dried red lentils and stock. Simmer for 5 mins, then stir in the chopped tomatoes, cauliflower florets and chickpeas. Simmer for a further 10 mins, or until the lentils are tender.

4   Meanwhile, place the flatbread in the oven and cook to pack instructions.

5   Stir through half of the coriander just before serving and sprinkle with the remaining coriander to garnish.

Per serving: 397 cals, 11g fat, 2.8g sat fat, 11g total sugars, 2.1g salt

Cook's tip
If you have any leftovers, you can turn them into a soup for lunch the next day. Simply heat with a little hot vegetable stock, leave to cool a little, whiz with a stick blender, then add more hot stock until you get your desired consistency.

Ready in 30 mins

Vegetable pad Thai

A Thai takeaway favourite, this version has fresh egg noodles mixed with vegetable, egg and peanuts, and an easy oriental-inspired sauce

Serves 4
Prep time: 15 mins
Cook time: 10-15 mins

1 tbsp groundnut oil

10 spring onions, trimmed and sliced on the diagonal

1 red chilli, deseeded and finely chopped

2 cloves garlic, crushed

200g pack Sainsbury's Tenderstem broccoli, sliced lengthways

Zest and juice of 1 lime, plus extra lime wedges to serve

2 tbsp light soy sauce

1 tbsp light brown soft sugar

2 tbsp fragrant Thai base by Sainsbury's

2 carrots, peeled and sliced into ribbons

200g beansprouts

60g peanuts, toasted and roughly chopped

½ x 31g pack fresh coriander by Sainsbury's, roughly chopped

410g pack fresh free range egg noodles by Sainsbury's (ready cooked)

2 medium eggs, beaten

1 In a large wok or frying pan, heat the oil and add the spring onions, chilli, garlic and broccoli, and cook for 5 mins.

2 Meanwhile, in a small bowl, mix the lime zest and juice, soy sauce, brown sugar and fragrant Thai base with 3 tbsp of water.

3 Stir the carrots, beansprouts, half of the peanuts, half of the coriander and the noodles into the pan and cook for 2 mins, then push everything to one side and add the eggs. When they have begun to set, break them up with a spoon, then mix them into the veg and noodles.

4 Add the sauce and stir well to make sure everything is evenly coated. Cook for 2 mins, then serve immediately with the remaining coriander and peanuts sprinkled over, and the extra lime wedges on the side.

Per serving: 429 cals, 18g fat, 3.1g sat fat, 14g total sugars, 1.4g salt

Ready in 40 mins

Warming winter quinoa & kale salad

Try this unusual salad for something a little different. Served while it's still warm, it's hearty enough to make a pleasing winter supper

Serves 4
Prep time: 10 mins
Cook time: 20 mins, plus cooling

1 tsp cumin seeds

200g quinoa

650ml vegetable stock, hot

200g bag Sainsbury's British curly leaf kale

60g toasted pine nuts

1 carrot, peeled and grated

50g raisins

½ red onion, finely sliced

Zest and juice of 1 lemon

1 tbsp balsamic vinegar

1 tbsp clear honey

2 tbsp olive oil

50g goats' cheese, crumbled

1 Heat the cumin seeds in a large saucepan for 1-2 mins, until fragrant. Stir in the quinoa and cover with the stock. Bring to a simmer and cook, half covered, for 18 mins or until tender. Stir the kale into the quinoa for the last 5 mins of the cooking time.

2 Put the quinoa and kale into a large bowl and allow to cool for 10 mins. Then stir in the pine nuts, carrot, raisins and red onion. Season with salt and freshly ground black pepper.

3 In a small bowl, mix together the lemon zest and juice, balsamic vinegar and honey. Slowly whisk in the oil. Pour over the salad and mix well. Serve with the goat's cheese crumbled over.

Per serving: 360 cals, 22g fat, 4.4g sat fat, 19g total sugars, 1.3g salt

Ready in 40 mins

Curried bubble & squeak with raita

Serves 4
Prep time: 15 mins
Cook time: 25 mins

A spicy version of a family favourite that's packed with tasty veg

300g pack Sainsbury's butternut squash & sweet potato, pierced with a fork

1 tbsp olive oil

15g unsalted butter

1 tsp cumin seeds

1 green chilli, deseeded and finely chopped

1 onion, finely chopped

½ x 240g pack ready trimmed Brussels sprouts by Sainsbury's, sliced

½ tsp ground coriander

½ tsp garam masala

3 cloves garlic, finely chopped

100g curly leaf kale, shredded

400g pack ready mashed potato by Sainsbury's

¼ x 31g pack fresh coriander by Sainsbury's, roughly chopped

150g tub Indian coriander & mint raita by Sainsbury's

1 Preheat the oven to 180°C, fan 160°C, gas 4. Meanwhile, cook the pack of butternut & sweet potato in the microwave on high for 4 mins, until tender.

2 Heat the olive oil and butter in a 22-24cm ovenproof frying pan and cook the cumin seeds and chilli for 2 mins, then add in the onion and Brussels sprouts. Cook for 5 mins, then stir in the ground coriander, garam masala, garlic and curly leaf kale. Cook for a further 5 mins.

3 Stir in the butternut and sweet potato and make sure everything is fully combined. Season with salt and freshly ground pepper. Spoon the mashed potato into the pan, and mixed it into the other veg. Cook for 5 mins over a low heat, then put the pan into the oven and cook for a further 5 mins. Serve garnished with chopped coriander and the raita.

Per serving: 246 cals, 9.4g fat, 3.7g sat fat, 11g total sugars, 0.47g salt

Cook's tip
Instead of using bought vegetables, you can use the same quantity of leftover veg. Carrots, parsnips, roast potatoes and spinach work equally well.

Serves 4
Prep time: 10 mins
Cook time: 30 mins

Ready in 40 mins

Roasted stuffed peppers

These red peppers filled with a tasty combination of rice, artichokes and feta cheese are simple to prepare, but look really impressive

4 large red peppers
250g pack microwaveable basmati rice by Sainsbury's
3 tbsp crème fraîche
5 spring onions, trimmed and finely chopped
2 cloves garlic, finely chopped
400g tin Sainsbury's artichoke hearts in water, drained and roughly chopped

Zest of 1 lemon
2 tbsp chopped fresh flat-leaf parsley, plus extra to garnish
100g feta cheese, crumbled
2 tbsp olive oil

1 Preheat the oven to 180°C, fan 160°C, gas 4.

2 Cut the peppers in half; if you can, leave some of the stalk on each piece, then scoop out the seeds and any white pith. Place in a non-stick roasting tin, with the cavities facing upwards.

3 Empty the rice into a large bowl and mix in the crème fraîche, spring onions, garlic, chopped artichoke hearts, lemon zest, chopped parsley and half of the feta. Season with salt and freshly ground black pepper, then spoon into the peppers, dividing the mixture evenly. Sprinkle the peppers with the remaining crumbled feta and drizzle a little olive oil over each pepper.

4 Bake for 30 mins or until sizzling hot and browning slightly. Serve with a sprinkling of chopped parsley to garnish.

Per serving: 324 cals, 17g fat, 8.4g sat fat, 12g total sugars, 0.58g salt

Serves 4
Prep time: 10 mins
Cook time: 30 mins

Ready in 40 mins

Aubergine curry

Fancy a curry that's packed with flavour, but not fat? This spicy dish is the perfect guilt-free Friday night treat

---

1 tbsp olive oil
1 onion, chopped
2 medium aubergines, trimmed and cut into 2cm cubes
1 tbsp medium curry powder
1 tsp cumin seeds
2cm piece fresh ginger, peeled and grated
1 tbsp tomato purée

2 x 400g tins Taste the Difference Pomodorini cherry tomatoes
410g tin chickpeas in water by Sainsbury's, drained and rinsed
200ml passata
2 x 250g packs microwaveable basmati rice by Sainsbury's
½ x 28g pack fresh basil by Sainsbury's, leaves picked, torn

---

1 Heat the oil in a deep frying pan over a medium heat. Add the onion and cook for 5 mins, then add the aubergines and cook for a further 10 mins. Stir in the curry powder, cumin seeds and ginger for the last 1 min.

2 Add the tomato purée, cherry tomatoes, chickpeas and passata, then simmer gently for 12-15 mins. Add a little water if necessary.

3 Meanwhile, cook the rice according to pack instructions.

4 Divide the curry and basmati rice between 4 bowls, and garnish with the basil to serve.

Per serving: 387 cals, 5.6g fat, 0.8g sat fat, 16.3g total sugars, 0.26g salt

Cook's tip
Get experimenting with microwaveable rice – it's a great time saving product. Wholegrain and pilau also work really well with this curry.

Serves 4
Prep time: 10 mins
Cook time: 40 mins

Ready in 50 mins

Leek & cheese frittata

Need an inspired fix for a light lunch or supper? This frittata is a great standby recipe, and a good way to get the kids to eat more veg, too

---

1 tbsp olive oil

1 onion, chopped

1 red chilli, deseeded and chopped

2 leeks, trimmed and sliced

6 large eggs

3 tbsp chopped fresh chives

80g extra mature British Cheddar, grated

150g frozen peas

560g tin peeled new potatoes by Sainsbury's, drained and halved

---

1 Preheat the grill to medium. Heat the olive oil in a 20-22cm non-stick, ovenproof frying pan over a low heat. Add the onion, chilli and leeks, and cook for 10 mins until the vegetables have started to soften.

2 In a separate bowl, beat the eggs, then add the chives and 50g of the Cheddar. Season with salt and freshly ground black pepper, then pour over the vegetables in the pan. Add the peas and stir to combine. Top with the halved potatoes and cook over a low heat for 10-15 mins.

3 Sprinkle over the remaining Cheddar and grill for 5-10 mins until the top of the fritatta is set and golden.

Per serving: 365 cals, 21g fat, 7.8g sat fat, 5.9g total sugars, 0.72g salt

Ready in 50 mins

Vegetable Thai green curry

A colourful array of veg is cooked in a spicy, coconut milk sauce and topped with coriander and cashew nuts

Serves 4
Prep time: 15 mins
Cook time: 35 mins

2 tbsp vegetable oil
1 onion, finely sliced
3 cloves garlic, sliced
1 tsp crushed chillies by Sainsbury's
½ x 31g pack fresh coriander by Sainsbury's, leaves and stalks separated and chopped
2cm piece fresh ginger, peeled and finely chopped
2 tbsp green Thai curry paste (suitable for vegetarians)

500g sweet potatoes, peeled and cut into 2cm cubes
400ml tin light coconut milk
175g pack babycorn & mange tout by Sainsbury's, the mange tout cut in half diagonally
1 courgette, trimmed and cut into 1cm rounds, then halved
60g cashew nuts, chopped
1 lime, halved

1 Heat the vegetable oil in a casserole over a medium heat. Add the onion, garlic, crushed chillies and chopped coriander stalks. Fry for 5 mins, until the onion is soft but not coloured. Stir in the fresh ginger, Thai curry paste and sweet potatoes, and cook for a further 2-3 mins.

2 Pour in the coconut milk with 300ml water and stir well. The coconut sauce should just cover the sweet potatoes, but don't worry if it doesn't. Bring to the boil, then reduce the heat, cover and simmer for 12 mins.

3 Add the babycorn and courgette, and continue to simmer for another 10 mins, adding in the mange tout for the final 2 mins. Ladle into bowls and garnish with the coriander leaves and chopped cashew nuts. Squeeze over lime juice to serve.

Per serving: 386 cals, 20g fat, 8.4g sat fat, 14g total sugars, 0.81g salt

Serves 4
Prep time: 15 mins
Cook time: 35-40 mins

Ready in 55 mins

Feta & vegetable pie

A tasty combination of spinach, carrots and feta - it's easy to make, too!
Using filo pasty gives the pie a lovely crispy top

1½ tbsp olive oil
½ x 220g pack (6 sheets) ready rolled
filo pastry by Sainsbury's
500g frozen chopped spinach
by Sainsbury's, defrosted
2 carrots, peeled and grated
28g pack fresh flat-leaf parsley
by Sainsbury's, chopped

1 tsp dried oregano
50g pine nuts
150g feta cheese, crumbled
3 medium eggs, lightly beaten
170g bag baby leaf Italian style peppery
salad by Sainsbury's

---

1 Preheat the oven to 200ºC, fan 180ºC, gas 6. Brush a deep, 20cm round, loose-bottomed cake tin with a little of the oil. Layer 3 sheets of filo in the base and up the sides of the tin, brushing each sheet with a little oil.

2 Squeeze any excess water out of the defrosted spinach. Put the spinach in a large bowl and stir in the carrots, parsley, oregano, pine nuts and feta. Add the eggs and season with salt and freshly ground black pepper. Mix well until combined.

3 Spoon the spinach mixture into the tin and fold the overhanging pastry over the top. Top with the remaining 3 sheets of filo, scrunching a little to fit the tin, and brushing the top of each with a little oil.

4 Bake for 35-40 mins, until golden and crisp, then cut into wedges and serve with the baby leaf salad on the side.

Per serving: 439 cals, 28.5g fat, 9.4g sat fat, 5.7g total sugars, 1.33g salt

‘ Everyone will love
this veggie pie with
its crunchy filo top ’

Serves 4
Prep time: 15 mins
Cook time: 40 mins

Ready in 55 mins

Ratatouille with goats' cheese crumb

An unusual addition to a traditional ratatouille, the goats' cheese gives this dish a deliciously savoury, creamy twist

5 tbsp olive oil
1 medium aubergine, trimmed and roughly chopped into 2cm cubes
1 red onion, roughly chopped
3 cloves garlic, roughly chopped
1 yellow pepper, deseeded and cut into thin strips
2 red peppers, deseeded and cut into thin strips
2 courgettes, trimmed and cut into 1cm rounds

2 x 390g cartons Italian chopped tomatoes, in tomato juice by Sainsbury's
1 tbsp dark brown soft sugar
1 tsp smoked paprika
50g fresh white breadcrumbs
2 tbsp fresh flat-leaf parsley, finely chopped
125g pack Abergavenny goats' cheese by Sainsbury's, crumbled
1/2 x 28g pack fresh basil, torn

1 Heat 2 tbsp oil in the base of a shallow, heavy-based casserole (about 1.5 litres) over a high heat. Add the aubergine and fry for 4-5 mins until starting to colour. Remove from the pan and set aside before adding 2 tbsp olive oil to the casserole. Add the onion, garlic and peppers and fry for 4-5 mins until the onion and peppers begin to soften slightly. Finally add the courgettes and continue to fry for 3-4 mins.

2 Return the aubergine to the casserole along with the chopped tomatoes, brown sugar and smoked paprika. Simmer for 20 mins, covered, until all the vegetables have softened.

3 Preheat the grill to high. In a small bowl, mix the breadcrumbs with the parsley and half of the goats' cheese. Stir the basil and remaining goats' cheese into the ratatouille, then scatter over the breadcrumbs. Drizzle with the remaining olive oil, then place under the grill for 5 mins until the top starts to turn golden. Serve immediately.

Per serving: 386 cals, 23g fat, 7.7g sat fat, 23g total sugars, 0.45g salt

Serves 6
Prep time: 15 mins
Cook time: 40 mins

Ready in 55 mins

Veg casserole with herb dumplings

Three different kinds of beans form the basis for this robust casserole, while the Italian cheese adds a Mediterranean touch to the little herb dumplings

1 tbsp olive oil
1 onion, roughly chopped
3 garlic cloves, roughly chopped
½ tsp crushed chillies by Sainsbury's
A few sprigs fresh rosemary, leaves removed and chopped
300g sweet potatoes, peeled and chopped into 1-2cm cubes
410g tin butter beans in water by Sainsbury's, rinsed and drained
410g tin red kidney beans in water by Sainsbury's, drained
410g tin black-eyed beans in water by Sainsbury's, drained
390g carton Italian chopped tomatoes in tomato juice by Sainsbury's
50g unsalted butter, chilled
125g self-raising flour
2 tbsp roughly chopped fresh flat-leaf parsley
50g basics Italian hard cheese, finely grated
200g cabbage (Savoy or green), sliced

1 Heat the olive oil in a 1.5 litre flameproof casserole and fry the onion, garlic and crushed chillies for 5 mins, stirring, until the onion begins to soften. Add the rosemary, sweet potatoes, all of the beans, the tomatoes and 200ml water, and stir well. Reduce the heat to low and simmer for 20 mins, covered, or until the sweet potato is almost cooked through. Stir occasionally to prevent it sticking to the base of the casserole and burning. Season with salt and freshly ground black pepper.

2 Meanwhile, make the dumplings. In a small bowl, rub the butter into the flour, then mix in the chopped parsley and cheese. Add 3 tbsp cold water and mix together so you have a soft dough. Divide into 12 small dumplings, each one about the size of a walnut.

3 Stir the cabbage into the stew, check the seasoning, then drop the dumplings onto the surface of the stew, spaced about 3cm apart. Cover (making sure the lid is at least 2.5cm above the stew so the dumplings have room to spread as they cook), and cook for 15 mins, until the dumplings puff up slightly. Serve immediately.

Per serving: 588 cals, 19g fat, 10g sat fat, 13g total sugars, 0.58g salt

Serves 4
Prep time: 15 mins
Cook time: 50 mins

Ready in 1 hour 5 mins

Broad bean & pea risotto

This tasty risotto is baked in the oven, so there's no need for lots of stirring. The goats' cheese adds a creamy flavour, while the lemon adds a fresh zing!

1 tbsp olive oil

1 onion, finely chopped,

2 cloves garlic, crushed

250g risotto rice by Sainsbury's

1 litre vegetable stock, hot

200ml semi-skimmed milk

100ml crème fraîche

28g pack fresh mint by Sainsbury's, finely chopped, reserving a few sprigs to garnish

Zest and juice of 1 lemon

300g frozen broad beans, defrosted and podded

200g frozen petits pois

200g pack sugar snap peas by Sainsbury's, sliced lengthways

½ x 125g pack Abergavenny goats' cheese by Sainsbury's

1 Preheat the oven to 180°C, 160°C fan, gas 4. Heat the oil in a large casserole, add the onion and cook for 5 mins, then add the garlic and cook for a further 2 mins. Stir in the rice and allow to cook for 2-3 mins.

2 Pour in the stock and milk, cover and cook in the oven for 20 mins. Take the casserole out of the oven, stir well, then return to the oven for another 15 mins or until the rice is almost cooked.

3 Remove from the oven and stir in the crème fraîche, most of the chopped mint, the lemon juice, broad beans, petits pois and sugar snaps, and return to the oven to cook for a final 5 mins.

4 Serve immediately with the goats' cheese crumbled over the top, garnished with the reserved mint leaves and lemon zest.

Per serving: 528 cals, 18g fat, 9.8g sat fat, 10g total sugars, 1.3g salt

Ready in 1 hour 10 mins

Rainbow vegetable & egg bake

Serves 4
Prep time: 20 mins
Cook time: 40-50 mins

A veggie version of a breakfast hash, this one-pan bake is a great meat-free meal. Vary the veg, if you like, depending on what you have in the fridge

1 tbsp olive oil
700g Maris Piper potatoes, peeled and finely diced
2 red onions, finely sliced
2 cloves garlic, finely chopped
2 carrots, peeled and grated
100g frozen garden peas

325g tin naturally sweet sweetcorn by Sainsbury's, drained
¼ x 20g pack fresh rosemary by Sainsbury's
1 courgette, trimmed and sliced into ribbons
50g mild British Cheddar
4 medium eggs

1 Preheat the oven to 180°C, fan 160°C, gas 4. Heat the oil in a large ovenproof frying pan and cook the potatoes for 15 mins until golden. Add the onions, garlic, carrots, peas, sweetcorn and rosemary. Cook for a further 15 mins.

2 Remove and discard the rosemary. Season the veg with salt and freshly ground black pepper, then scatter over the courgette ribbons and Cheddar. Using the back of a spoon, create 4 small wells in the mixture. Break the eggs into the wells, then transfer to the oven. Bake for 10 mins or until the egg whites have set and the yolk is runny*. If you'd prefer set yolks, bake for 15-20 mins. Remove from the oven and serve.

Per serving: 397 cals, 14g fat, 4.9g sat fat, 15g total sugars, 0.46g salt

*Cook's note: this recipe contains partially cooked egg.

puddings

Ready in 25 mins

Marmalade choc-chip pudding

Serves 6
Prep time: 5 mins
Cook time: 20 mins

Ⓥ

This twist on a bread and butter pudding combines the classic flavours of chocolate and orange. Using ready-made custard makes it very quick, too

10 choc chip brioche swirls
3 tbsp good quality orange marmalade
500g pot Taste the Difference
Madagascan vanilla custard

20g smooth dark chocolate
by Sainsbury's, grated

1 Preheat the oven to 180°C, fan 160°C, gas 4. Spread the brioche rolls with the marmalade.

2 Pour half the custard into the bottom of a 1.5-litre ovenproof baking dish. Place the brioche rolls on top of the custard, arranging them so they stand upright.

3 Pour over the remaining custard and sprinkle over the grated chocolate. Bake in the oven for 20 mins, until golden on top.

Per serving: 460 cals, 20g fat, 11g sat fat, 35g total sugars, 0.63g salt

Poached pears & raspberries

Heat 1 litre apple & pear juice drink by Sainsbury's, 50g caster sugar and a vanilla pod, halved, in a pan. Add 4 peeled, halved and cored pears, then simmer gently for 10-15 mins, until nearly soft. Remove the pears and boil the liquid for 5-10 mins until reduced by half to a syrup. Stir in 200g fresh or frozen raspberries, then cook for a further 2 mins. Drizzle over the pears and serve with a spoonful of natural Greek yogurt.

Serves 4 Ready: 35 mins Prep time: 5 mins Cook time: 30 mins

Per serving: 280 cals, 2.6g fat, 1.3g sat fat, 59g total sugars, 0.06g salt

Serves 4
Prep time: 10 mins
Cook time: 20-25 mins

V

Ready in 35 mins

Apple & pear crumbles

A classic pudding that's delicious on its own or served with creamy custard

---

65g plain flour
25g unsalted butter, chilled,
cut into pieces
50g light brown soft sugar
2 pears, peeled, cored and sliced

2 cooking apples, peeled, cored and sliced
100g raisins
½ tsp cinnamon
Zest and juice of 1 lemon

---

1 Preheat the oven to 180°C, fan 160°C, gas 4. Put the flour and butter into a food processor and pulse to crumbs, then stir in 30g of the sugar. If you don't have a processor, put the flour into a large mixing bowl, add the butter and rub it in lightly, using your fingertips. When it's crumbly, add the sugar and combine.

2 In a large bowl, mix together the pears, apples, raisins, cinnamon, lemon zest and juice, the remaining sugar and 100ml water. Divide the mixture between 4 x 150ml ramekins. Spoon over the crumble mixture, then bake for 20-25 mins, until the crumble is golden on top and the fruit is tender.

Per serving: 287 cals, 5.7g fat, 3.1g sat fat, 43g total sugars, 0.05g salt

Cook's tip
If you prefer, this can also be cooked as one large dessert. Add another 15 mins onto the cooking time and check the fruit is tender. It may need a little longer, depending on the ripeness of the fruit.

Serves 8
Prep time: 15 mins
Cook time: 15 mins,
plus cooling

Ready in 50 mins

Tiramisu roulade

The famous coffee trifle pud is transformed into a tempting sponge roll

½ tsp oil, for greasing
3 medium eggs
175g light brown soft sugar
1 tbsp instant coffee, dissolved in 1 tbsp hot water
2 tbsp ground almonds
60g self-raising flour

1 tbsp cocoa powder
250g tub mascarpone by Sainsbury's
150ml pot single cream by Sainsbury's
1 tsp vanilla extract
1 tbsp coffee liqueur (optional)
25g dark chocolate, grated

1 Preheat the oven to 180°C, fan 160°C, gas 4. Grease and line a 32cm x 23cm Swiss roll tin with baking parchment, making sure the paper comes up above the sides of the tray by 2cm.

2 Whisk the eggs and 150g of the sugar with an electric hand whisk for 5 mins, until thick and light. Fold in the coffee mixture, ground almonds and flour, then pour into the tin, spreading the mixture into the corners.

3 Bake for 15 mins, until golden and springy. Remove from the oven and turn out onto another piece of baking parchment, dusted with cocoa powder. With the shortest side facing you, roll the sponge up inside the paper and set aside to cool completely – about 20 mins.

4 Meanwhile, whisk together the mascarpone, cream, remaining sugar, vanilla extract and coffee liqueur (if using), until light and thick.

5 When the sponge is cool, unroll it, spoon on the filling and spread it over the sponge, leaving a 2cm border at the edges. Roll the sponge back up, leaving the baking parchment behind. Slide onto a plate and sprinkle over the grated chocolate to serve.

Per serving: 347 cals, 22g fat, 13g sat fat, 26g total sugars, 0.2g salt

Cook's tip
If you like a stronger coffee flavour, add another 2 tsp of instant coffee to the coffee and water mixture when making the sponge.

Ready in 50 mins

Blackberry clafoutis

Serves 4
Prep time: 10 mins
Cook time: 35-40 mins

Traditionally made with cherries, this version of the impressive but easy-to-make batter pudding makes the most of autumnal blackberries

10g unsalted butter, for greasing
40g plain flour
30g caster sugar
2 medium eggs

200ml semi-skimmed milk
½ tbsp sunflower oil
225g fresh blackberries, washed
Icing sugar, for dusting

1 Preheat the oven to 180ºC, fan 160ºC, gas 4. Grease a shallow, 1-litre ovenproof tart or flan dish with the butter.

2 Sift the flour into a bowl, then stir in the sugar. Whisk in the eggs, one at a time. Slowly add the milk to create a smooth batter. Stir in the sunflower oil and mix well.

3 Arrange the blackberries in the base of the dish, then pour over the batter. Bake in the centre of the oven for 35-40 mins, until golden on top and a skewer comes out clean from the centre. Dust with icing sugar to serve.

Per serving: 187 cals, 7.6g fat, 2.7g sat fat, 14g total sugars, 0.18g salt

Crumble-topped baked peaches

Preheat the oven to 180ºC, fan 160ºC, gas 4. Halve and de-stone 4 peaches and place into a small shallow baking dish, cut sides up. Pour in 150ml white wine with 1 halved vanilla pod. In a food processor, whiz together 50g unsalted butter with 50g plain flour, until it resembles breadcrumbs. Stir in 30g light brown soft sugar and 30g grated marzipan, then spoon onto the peaches. Bake for 30 mins, until the peaches are soft and the top is crisp. Serve with the syrup from the tin and some crème fraîche.

Serves 4 Ready: 40 mins Prep time: 10 mins Cook time: 30 mins

Per serving: 305 cals, 18g fat, 11g sat fat, 22g total sugars, 0.01g salt

Ready in 55 mins

Apple tarte tatin

Serves 8
Prep time: 10 mins
Cook time: 35 mins,
plus cooling

A classic French dessert that looks so mouthwatering when turned out of its dish. Try serving it warm with a scoop of ice cream, or a drizzle of cream

---

375g pack ready rolled light puff pastry by Sainsbury's
50g unsalted butter
100g dark brown soft sugar
1/2 ball stem ginger, finely chopped

2 tbsp ginger syrup (from the stem ginger jar)
600g Granny Smith apples (about 7 small ones), peeled, cored and halved

---

1 Preheat the oven to 220°C, fan 200°C, gas 7.

2 Cut a 26cm circle (use a plate or cake tin as a guide) from the pastry, then place it in the fridge to chill while you make the rest of the tart.

3 Over a medium heat, melt the butter in a 26cm ovenproof frying pan and add the sugar, stirring to remove any lumps, then add the stem ginger and ginger syrup. Shake the pan gently but do not stir, and allow the mixture to bubble for 1 min.

4 Arrange the apples, round side facing the bottom of the pan, on top of the caramel in a spiral pattern. Cover with the prepared pastry circle, tucking the edges inside the pan around the apples.

5 Place in the oven and bake for 30 mins or until the pastry is golden brown and puffed up.

6 Remove from the oven and leave to cool for 10 mins, then place a serving plate over the pan and flip over as quickly and smoothly as you can. Serve the tart warm in slices with a little crème fraîche, if you like.

Per serving: 301 cals, 13g fat, 6.6g sat fat, 24g total sugars, 0.3g salt

Ready in 1 hour

Sticky chocolate pudding

Serves 6
Prep time: 10 mins
Cook time: 30-35 mins, plus cooling

V

Not too heavy, not too light – this gooey chocolate pud's just right. Making it in one dish is great for sharing, but you could also make individual puds

150g dark chocolate, broken into pieces

150g unsalted butter, cubed

200g caster sugar

3 medium eggs, beaten

50g ground almonds

50g self-raising flour

Icing sugar, for dusting

1 Preheat the oven to 180ºC, fan 160ºC, gas 4. Put the chocolate, butter and sugar in a microwaveable mixing bowl and place in the microwave. Cook on low for 4 mins, stirring every 1 min to check.

2 Stir in the beaten eggs, ground almonds and the flour. Tip into a 1.5-litre ovenproof dish and bake for 25-30 mins. It should still be gooey inside.

3 Allow to cool slightly (about 15 mins), then dust with icing sugar just before serving.

Per serving: 583 cals, 36.7g fat, 20g sat fat, 48.3g total sugars, 0.17g salt

Cook's tip
As this is quite a rich, indulgent pudding, serve it with a dollop or two of reduced-fat crème fraîche or some Greek-style yogurt if you like.

This will come out of the oven all lovely and gooey!

Serves 8
Prep time: 5 mins
Cook time: 1 hour
10 mins

Ready in 1 hour 15 mins

Berry rice pudding

A classic pud with a fruity addition. Using pudding rice gives it a really soft, creamy texture – the perfect comfort food for autumn evenings

200g pudding rice
75g light brown soft sugar
1.2 litres whole milk
1 vanilla pod, split in half and seeds scraped out

150g blackberries
150g raspberries

1 Preheat the oven to 150°C, fan 130°C, gas 2. Put the rice, 50g sugar, the milk and the vanilla seeds and pod in a medium, shallow, heavy-bottomed, ovenproof pan (about 1.5 litre) and bring to a gentle simmer, stirring often. Cook for 10 mins.

2 Place in the oven and cook for 1 hour. Stir in the berries and sprinkle the remaining sugar over the top 15 mins before the end of the cooking time.

3 Remove from the oven, take out the vanilla pod and serve.

Per serving: 232 cals, 5.7g fat, 3.5g sat fat, 18g total sugars, 0.23g salt

Serves 12
Prep time: 15 mins
Cook time: 55 mins,
plus cooling

Ready in 1 hour 20 mins

Mango & pineapple freeform pie

You don't need a special pie dish to make this delicious tropical fruit dessert – just assemble it all on a baking sheet and pop it into the oven

500g shortcrust pastry block by Sainsbury's
1 tbsp plain flour
1 medium egg, beaten
2 tbsp semolina
2 tbsp desiccated coconut

480g pack frozen mango chunks by Sainsbury's, defrosted
400g pack pineapple pieces by Sainsbury's
Zest of 2 limes and juice of 1 lime
3 tbsp granulated sugar

1 Preheat the oven to 200°C, fan 180°C, gas 6. Roll the pastry into a circle, 5mm thick and place on a floured baking tray.

2 Brush the pastry with half the egg, leaving a 7cm border. Sprinkle the semolina, then the coconut, onto the brushed egg.

3 In a bowl, mix together the mango, pineapple, lime zest, juice and 2 tbsp sugar. Spread the mixture evenly over the coconut, then lift the pastry border over the fruit to hold it in.

4 Brush the pastry with the remaining egg and sprinkle with the remaining 1 tbsp sugar. Bake for 55 mins, until golden. Allow to cool for 10 mins on the tray before serving.

Per serving: 325 cals, 18g fat, 8g sat fat, 13g total sugars, 0.33g salt

Cook's tip
Make this extra-special by served with a scoop of ice cream or a dollop of crème fraîche.

Serves 8
Prep time: 10-15 mins
Cook time: 2 hours,
plus standing

Ready in 2 hours 20 mins

Lemon & blueberry steamed sponge

A lovely traditional steamed pud to serve on a chilly autumnal day

150g unsalted butter
165g lemon curd
150g white caster sugar
3 medium eggs

175g self-raising flour
150g blueberries, tossed together
with 1 tsp flour

1 Butter a 1.2 litre pudding basin, spoon 90g of the lemon curd into the bottom and set aside. Make a pleat in a large rectangle of foil and a large rectangle of baking parchment. Grease the baking parchment with a little of the butter and set aside.

2 In a mixing bowl, whisk the remaining butter and lemon curd together with the sugar until light and fluffy. Beat in the eggs with a spoonful of the flour, then fold in the remaining flour and half of the blueberries.

3 Spoon half of the mixture into the basin and scatter over the remaining blueberries. Top with the remaining sponge mixture, then cover the basin with the pleated foil and baking parchment and seal it tightly around the lip of the basin with kitchen string, ensuring the pudding is water tight.

4 Put the pudding into a steamer over a pan of boiling water or place on a plate in a deep pan with boiling water coming halfway up the sides. Cover and cook on a low simmer for 2 hours. Carefully remove the basin from the pan and leave for 5 mins, then slide a knife around the sides and carefully turn out the pudding onto a serving plate. Take care as the hot lemon curd drizzles down over the top. Serve with a little crème fraîche, if you like.

Per serving: 417 cals, 22g fat, 13g sat fat, 31g total sugars, 0.38g salt

> ### Cook's tip
> Short on time? Follow the recipe above and, when you're ready to cook the pud, cover the basin with greased cling film and pierce a couple of times. Cook in the microwave on high (900W) for 7½ mins, and let it sit for 3-4 mins before turning out, as above.

Serves 8
Prep time: 5 mins
Cook time: 1 hour 10
mins, plus cooling
and chilling

Ready in 3 hours 30 mins

Baked custard & summer fruits

A lovely chilled dessert that combines creamy custard with sharp, fruity berries. Make it well ahead of time to allow for it to set in the fridge

300g frozen summer fruits, defrosted and excess liquid drained off
125g caster sugar
4 medium egg yolks

Pinch of freshly grated nutmeg
Few drops Sainsbury's Taste the Difference Madagascan vanilla extract
300ml pot double cream by Sainsbury's

1 Preheat the oven to 160°C, fan 140°C, gas 3. Place the berries in a 1.5-litre baking dish with 25g of the sugar and cook for 10 mins in the oven until they have heated up.

2 Beat the egg yolks, remaining sugar, nutmeg, vanilla extract and cream in a bowl with an electric whisk, for 2-3 mins, until smooth. Pour the mixture over the fruit - do this by pouring it over a spoon to ensure it drops down gently, so the custard doesn't get mixed up with the berries. Place the dish into a roasting tin and pour nearly boiling water into the tin until it comes halfway up the side of the dish.

3 Bake on the bottom shelf of the oven for 1 hour, until the custard is set around the edges but still wobbly in the middle. Remove from the oven, set aside to cool and place into the fridge for 2 hours to set up fully. Remove from the fridge and serve, either chilled or at room temperature.

Per serving: 272 cals, 21g fat, 12g sat fat, 18g total sugars, 0.01g salt

Cook's tip
You could also use fresh fruit instead of frozen: use the same quantity, but cook it in a pan for 5-10 mins with the sugar until softened, then spoon into a baking dish and continue the recipe as above. Try any summer berries, or rhubarb and orange zest.

Find the right recipe at a glance

All recipes have been tried, tested and tasted by Sainsbury's, so you can be sure of great results every time

Index

Conversion table

Weights		Volume		Measurements		Oven temperatures		
							fan	gas
15g	½oz	25ml	1fl oz	2mm	1/16in	110°C	90°C	
25g	1oz	50ml	2fl oz	3mm	⅛in	120°C	100°C	½
40g	1½oz	75ml	3fl oz	4mm	⅙in	140°C	120°C	1
50g	2oz	100ml	4fl oz	5mm	¼in	150°C	130°C	2
60g	2½oz	150ml	5fl oz (¼pint)	1cm	½in	160°C	140°C	3
75g	3oz	175ml	6fl oz	2cm	¾in	180°C	160°C	4
100g	3½oz	200ml	7fl oz	2.5cm	1in	190°C	170°C	5
125g	4oz	225ml	8fl oz	3cm	1¼in	200°C	180°C	6
150g	5oz	250ml	9fl oz	4cm	1½in	220°C	200°C	7
175g	6oz	300ml	10fl oz (½pint)	4.5cm	1¾in	230°C	210°C	8
200g	7oz	350ml	13fl oz	5cm	2in	240°C	220°C	9
225g	8oz	400ml	14fl oz	6cm	2½in			
250g	9oz	450ml	16fl oz (¾pint)	7.5cm	3in			
275g	10oz	600ml	20fl oz (1 pint)	9cm	3½in			
300g	11oz	750ml	25fl oz (1¼pints)	10cm	4in			
350g	12oz	900ml	30fl oz (1½pints)	13cm	5in			
375g	13oz	1 litre	34fl oz (1¾pints)	13.5cm	5¼in			
400g	14oz	1.2 litres	40fl oz (2 pints)	15cm	6in			
425g	15oz	1.5 litres	52fl oz (2½pints)	16cm	6½in			
450g	1lb	1.8 litres	60fl oz (3 pints)	18cm	7in			
500g	1lb 2oz			19cm	7½in			
650g	1lb 7oz			20cm	8in			
675g	1½lb			23cm	9in			
700g	1lb 9oz			24cm	9½in			
750g	1lb 11oz			25.5cm	10in			
900g	2lb			28cm	11in			
1kg	2lb 4oz			30cm	12in			
1.5kg	3lb 6oz			32.5cm	13in			
				35cm	14in			

Always wash hands thoroughly after handling raw meat. Wash vegetables, fruit and fresh herbs before use. Public health advice is to avoid consumption of raw or lightly cooked eggs, especially for those vulnerable to infection, including pregnant women, babies and the elderly.

seven.co.uk

© Produced by Seven Publishing on behalf of Sainsbury's Supermarkets Ltd, 33 Holborn, London EC1N 2HT.
Published September 2013. All rights reserved. No part of this publication may be reproduced, stored in a retrieval system or transmitted in any form by any means, electronic, mechanical, photocopying, recording or otherwise, without the prior written permission of Seven Publishing. Printed and bound by Butler Tanner & Dennis Ltd, Frome and London. ISBN-13: 978-0-9566303-8-4

Credits

Food
Food editor Hannah Yeadon
Food assistant Lottie Covell
Recipes & food styling Sophie Austen-Smith, Angela Drake, Georgina Fuggle, Sal Henley, Mima Sinclair, Joy Skipper

Design
Senior art director David Jenkins
Art director Nina Christopher
Stylist Morag Farquhar

Editorial
Editors Ward Hellewell, Julie Stevens

Account management
Account executive Jo Brennan
Consultant Lynne de Lacy
Client director Andy Roughton
Head of content Helen Renshaw

Photography
Photography Mike Hart
Additonal photography
Terry Benson, Craig Fordham, Dan Jones, William Lingwood, Gareth Morgans, Charlie Richards, Craig Robertson, Sam Stowell
Additional food stylists
Angela Boggiano, Fergal Connolly, Catherine Hill, Lucy McKelvie, Bianca Nice, Mari Williams
Additional stylists
Jenny Iggleden, Robert Merrett

For Sainsbury's
Book team Phil Carroll, Mavis Sarfo
Nutrition Annie Denny

Print & production
Production manager Mike Lamb
Colour origination Altaimage Ltd
Printers Butler Tanner & Dennis Ltd, Frome and London

Special thanks to...
Patricia Baker, Angela Romeo

seven.co.uk

FSC
www.fsc.org
MIX
Paper from responsible sources
FSC® C023561

GREAT BRITISH BOOKS
PUBLISHED & PRINTED IN THE UK